GLOBAL WAR AGAINST KAFFIRS

RISE OF THE ISLAMIC STATE

GLOBAL WAR AGAINST KAFFIRS

RISE OF THE ISLAMIC STATE

Ram Kumar Ohri, IPS (Retd.)

ZORBA BOOKS

Published in India by Zorba Books, 2016

Website: www.zorbabooks.com
Email: info@zorbabooks.com

Copyright © Ram Kumar Ohri

ISBN Print Book - 978-93-85020-80-3
ISBN eBook – 978-93-85020-81-0

These are the authors views and he has made every effort to ensure the accuracy and completeness of information contained in this book, we assume no responsibility for errors, inaccuracies, omissions, or any inconsistencies herein. Any slights on people, places, or organizations are unintentional.

Zorba Books Pvt. Ltd. (opc)
Gurgaon, INDIA

Printed in India

Dedicated to my sweet granddaughters, Saloni and Jaisal and my soulmate, Pushpa.

Contents

Acknowledgements

This study into the growth of the savage phenomenon known as Islamic State has been in progress for more than 21 months. It has been a long journey and completing this manuscript would have been 'mission impossible' without the inspiration provided by my friend Ravi Ranjan Singh and enormous help of my daughter, Shivani. I was prompted into undertaking this research by a presentation organized by my friend Ravi of Live Values Foundation to highlight the plight of Yazidis – a hapless community thrown to wolves by the callous civil society. On 12 September, 2014, Ravi, a true 'Guru ka Sikh', had organized an event in New Delhi at the Press Club of India to highlight the frightful persecution of Yazidis by the newly created Islamic State. A young Yazidi student, codenamed 'Bablu' whose face was masked to protect his identity, gave a graphic account of the manslaughter of thousands of innocents and the sexual abuse heaped on the Yazidi womenfolk by the barbarians. The soul-searing event was ignored by the mainstream English media for reasons best left unstated. I, however, decided to undertake a study of the gruesome situation developing in West Asia.

I owe a debt of gratitude to my daughter, Shivani, for forwarding a down loaded copy of the book, *Management of Savagery* to me, written by Abu Bakr Naji, the ideologue of the Caliphate – an important source material. She continued to mail to me a host of invaluable inputs updating me from time to time about the toeholds developed by the ISIS in West Bengal, Bangladesh and several South Indian States. She also alerted me to the threat posed by the deep roots struck by the Islamic State in the Maldives.

I must also place on record my gratitude to Ms. Veryan Khan, Editorial Director of the Terrorism Research and Analysis Consortium

(TRAC), for alerting me to the dangerous plan of Islamic State to strike roots in faraway Brazil, in a bid to destabilize the South American continent. This is a startling development which could have posted a serious security threat to the Olympic Games being held in Rio, the capital of Brazil, in August, 2016.

Before concluding I must place on record my sincerest thanks to my wife, Pushpa, for putting up with my disorganized work schedule and the unkempt spectacle of my room. She tolerated all that with a smile and encouraged me to carry on with my writing schedule.

Introduction

For more than three decades India has been targeted by multiple Jihadi outfits, mostly floated by Pakistan and financially supported by Gulf petro-dollars. Historically, even before India was partitioned, the avowed goal of the Muslim leaders of India was to Islamize the entire sub-continent and write '*finis*' to the Hindu identity of India. This resolve of the Indian Muslim League was elucidated by Chaudhry Rahmat Ali in his notoriously famous '*Millat and Mission Statement*' issued in the year 1942. The resolution demanding the creation of Pakistan as a homeland for the Muslims of the sub-continent was moved by Chaudhry Rahmat Ali, a close associate of Mohammed Ali Jinnah and Sir Mohammed Iqbal, in the 29th annual session of the Muslim League in 1940. Rahmat Ali also formulated and circulated a statement of the goals to be attained by the Muslims in general, and the Pakistanis in particular, which was titled "*The Millat and the Mission Statement*". That mission statement of Rahmat Ali contained '*Seven Commandments of Destiny*' which made a frightening reading.

One of the long term objectives enunciated by Chaudhary Rahmat Ali was to convert the sub-continent of India into the continent of "*Dinia*" which he suggested should ultimately form a part of a bigger orbit called *Pakasia*'. He emphatically argued that Muslims "must write *finis* to the most deceptive fiction in the world that India is the sphere of Indianism".[1]

In recent times the jihadi threat to non-Muslim countries, including India, has multiplied manifold due to certain geostrategic developments caused by the formation of Islamic State in Iraq, Syria, Levant and several countries, including large tracts of the African continent. The radical menace extends right up to Indonesia and the

Philippines. To add fuel to the jihadi fire, several anti-India outfits operating from Afghanistan and Pakistan, acting in unison with the fifth columnists embedded in India are reported to be preparing for launching multiple terrorist strikes beginning from the state of Jammu & Kashmir in north and extending to West Bengal in the east and Kerala-Karnataka in the south. They have already established a bridgehead in Assam and West Bengal which led to multiple bomb blasts in Burdwan in October, 2014, with the complicity of Jamaat-ul-Mujahideen Bangladesh.

To give a turbo-push to the ongoing onslaught of radical Islam against all kaffir (non-believer) nations, Islamic State has issued multiple threats against India on the ground that it is a nation of kaffir Hindus where Muslims are persecuted. These developments have added a new dimension to the growing threat of jihadi terrorism across India. Every militant movement needs a charismatic hero, a high profile role model. At the time of the Russo-Afghan war of 1980s Osama bin Laden appeared on the scene to lead the Islamic warriors on their long march. Now a new Islamic icon, Abu Bakr al-Baghdadi of ISIS, has emerged as the newest warrior of radical Islam carrying the black banner of the Prophet. By virtue of being Caliph he could also be called the new leader of Islam who has established his rule by force of arms in a vast area of Syria, Iraq, Levant and several parts of the African continent.

The single-point agenda of ISIS is to Islamize the entire world and convert it into Dar-ul-Islam. At least in theory the anointment of Al-Baghdadi as Caliph Ibrahim, i.e. the master messiah of all Muslims of the world, has made him far more powerful than the Al-Qaeda leader Ayman al-Zawahiri. While quoting copiously from Islamic scriptures to justify their actions and to entice new recruits the ISIS have been beheading a number of captured westerners on camera. They have also captured thousands of Christian and Yazidi women for sex slavery. In one of the beheading videos the jihadi warriors cited two verses *verbatim* from the Quran, namely the Ayats 8.12 and 47.4 to rebut all those who claim that according to the Prophet, beheadings were cruel and unlawful.

The latest geopolitical developments like the emergence of Wilayat Khorasan in the AFPAK region and attempts of ISIS to create another Affiliate called 'Wilayat Hind' for conquering India are alarming signals. The concept of creating a mini-caliphate called Wilayat Hind highlights the danger of major faultline conflicts erupting in several parts of India under the umbrella of Islamic State. Frankly, the time has come to acknowledge that several Islamic outfits, including ISIS, Al Qaeda, Lashkar-e-Tayeba, Indian Mujahideen and Jaish-e-Muhammad aided by the ISI of Pakistan have cast their shadowy web in several States of India. The chance discovery of their nefarious subversion plot of October, 2014, in Burdwan, West Bengal, to stage multiple bomb blasts, showed the extent to which the unity and sovereignty of India has been compromised by Islamic groups. The discovery of close association between the Jamaat-ul Mujahideen Bangladesh (JMB) and the ultra-radical Muslim groups of West Bengal, is a typical example of eastern India morphing into the soft underbelly of India.

The investigations into the serial bomb blasts of 2014 in Burdwan by the National Investigation Agency revealed that nearly two dozen members of the Jamaat-ul Mujahideen Bangladesh and Indian Mujahideen were involved in the conspiracy to destabilize West Bengal. Four of them turned out to be Bangladeshi saboteurs operating in India. While 13 out of the 21 members of the conspiracy are in jail, the remaining eight, including three Bangladeshi militants, are on the run.

The charge sheet filed by the National Investigation Agency in May 2015, against 21 Muslim militants, claimed that JMB has been operating in eastern India in cahoots with the Indian Mujahideen. They have established a terror network in many districts including

Murshidabad, Nadia, Malda, Birbhum and Burdwan in West Bengal; Barpeta in Assam; and Sahibganj and Pakur in Jharkhand. The charge sheets revealed that a network of terrorist training camps were operating from selected madrasas and other hideouts, where handpicked youth were indoctrinated in jihadology and trained to unleash violence using explosives and firearms. There are strong reasons to believe that JMB is associated with the ISIS.

There are reports that during the last two years, several Muslim youth have been recruited by Islamic State from Maharashtra, West Bengal, Telangana, Andhra Pradesh, Kerala, Tamil Nadu, Karnataka and the Kashmir valley. They were allegedly being trained in Pakistan, Iraq and Syria to fight as 'fedayeen' of Islamic State. In an article published on January 24, 2015, in *The Sunday Indian*, New Delhi, Prof. M D Nalapat revealed that the number of the Indian Muslims joining the jihad-waging battalions of al-Baghdadi was nearly one thousand. According to Prof. Nalapat, ISIS recruiters have been working overtime in Uttar Pradesh, Assam, West Bengal, Kerala, Andhra Pradesh, Telangana and Maharashtra. There is, however, no official confirmation of the actual number of Indians fighting for ISIS in West Asia. Meanwhile, the ISIS mouthpiece, *Dabiq*, has claimed that nearly two lakh seventy thousand Indian Muslims continue to be regular viewers of their websites. This shows the huge reach already established by ISIS in India.

The phenomenon of Indian Muslims joining ISIS set alarm bells ringing in India's intelligence agencies after the case of Mumbai-based engineering student Arif Ejaz Majeed (also referred to as Areeb Majeed) came to light in November, 2014. Earlier in August 2014 it had been reported that Majeed had been killed while fighting alongside Islamist insurgents in Iraq. The death of the 23-year-old Majeed and the online tributes paid on his martyrdom by the Islamic outfit Ansar-ul-Tawhid (AuT) and activists of ISIS confirmed that a section of Indian youth had been persuaded to wage jihad, perhaps tempted by the lure of 72 houris in paradise. In reality, however, Arif Majeed did not die while waging jihad in the Islamic State. He returned to Mumbai in the last week of November. 2014, and was arrested by the Mumbai police on 28th November, 2014.

The confirmation of Arif Majeed's participation in the jihad waged by the ISIS punctured Indian media's routinely propagated bogey that only impoverished and marginalized Muslim youth wanted to join terror outfits like ISIS and the Indian Mujahideen. Majeed's case demonstrated that there is no truth in the frequently mouthed *alibi* parroted by self-styled secularists that poverty is the cause of a spurt in growth in radical Muslims. He comes from a well-to-do family. Only after the return of Majeed did the Indian intelligence agencies realize the enormity of the threat posed by Islamic State, making inroads into the mindscapes of Indian Muslims.

AuT's website has been repeatedly exhorting Indian Muslims to join the ongoing jihad. Time has come to admit that Islamic terror outfits have made aggressive inroads in several States. Al Isabah Media, an outfit working for the ISIS, has provided links to nine anti-Indian videos, the first of which was posted around the 3rd week of January, 2015. Another provocative video featuring the Canadian fighter Abu Muslim Kanadi was circulated in the beginning of February, 2015.

Nearly seven million Indians are working in the west Asian countries, e.g., Saudi Arabia, Yemen, United Arab Emirates, Kuwait and Iraq. There are reports that many of them have been joining the jihad-waging foot-soldiers of Islamic State.

The chief of Islamic State, Al-Baghdadi, has been openly targeting India through videos posted on Internet and audio messages relayed from time to time. In an audio message released during the holy month Ramzan in 2014, Al-Baghdadi claimed that several Indians were fighting shoulder to shoulder with the Chinese, American, French and German soldiers of the ISIS.

In one of his speeches Al-Baghdadi proclaimed that India was one of the countries where the rights of Muslims were violated. He also criticized the West for not condemning the killing of Muslims in Burma, Kashmir, Indonesia and in the Philippines.

According to intelligence agencies, the potential for recruitment of Muslim youth by ISIS from India is huge because of the country's large Muslim population. All jihadi recruits may not come from within India itself. Many could be a part of the working class diaspora in West Asia, where they come in contact with Muslims from other nations and get radicalized. Indians going for the annual Haj pilgrimage might add to the rising numbers.

Chapter 1

Caliphate is Reborn

"We took it forcibly at the point of a blade.
We brought it back conquered and compelled.
We established it in defiance of many.
And the people's necks were violently struck,
With bombings, explosions, and destruction,
And soldiers that do not see hardship as being difficult,
And lions that are thirsty in battle,
Having greedily drunk the blood of kufr [infidel].
Our khilāfah has indeed returned with certainty"

– From Declaration of the Caliphate titled
"This is the Promise of Allah", made on June 29,
2014, by Islamic State's spokesman, Al-Adnani.

The Islamic State led by Abu Bakr al-Baghdadi, initially dubbed by western media as another misadventure of jihadi zealots, has now grown into much more than a militant organization. It has rapidly evolved into a global politico-religious force commandeering a new country located in West Asia. Establishing Darul Islam across the world by waging global jihad is its cherished goal.

Historical Evolution of Caliphate

After capturing power in 1924, the revolutionary Turkish leader Kemal Ataturk officially abolished the Ottoman caliphate which was the supreme ecclesiastical authority for the Islamic fraternity called Ummah. The change led to far reaching political reforms in Turkey and the secularization of the Turkish nation. In recent years, however, Turkey has been sliding back into becoming a fundamentalist Islamic nation.

The Ottoman caliphate was a relic of Islam's glorious past. It was deemed as a continuation of the earlier caliphates starting from the times of the first four Rashidun Caliphs (i.e., the rightly-guided four caliphs), who ruled immediately after Prophet Muhammad's death in the seventh century. The seats of the four Rashidun caliphs were Medina and Mecca in Saudi Arabia, not in Turkey. By associating themselves with the history of the earlier Caliphates, the Ottoman royal family assumed the title of Caliph in the 14th century. Sultan Murad I was the first Ottoman Caliph who ruled from 1326 A.D. to 1389 A.D. and conquered the Balkans. He was stabbed to death by a Serbian nobleman during the battle of Kosovo.

The Islamic State, declared by the militant group formerly known as the ISIS or ISIL, is thus the first, and so far the only, bold attempt to resurrect the medieval system of governance of the early Muslim era by transplanting it in modern times. The Caliphate is a system of government considered by the believers to be a divinely sanctioned religious authority which invests unlimited religious and temporal power in the hands of the Caliph. By religious tradition the Caliph has the sole authority to enforce Sharia and interpret the scriptural texts. He is endowed with full religious and political jurisdiction over the entire Ummah, or the global nation of Islam. Among other things, the caliph has the authority to call for jihad against infidels which all Muslims are bound to follow. In a nutshell, for centuries the Caliphate has been a politico-religious concept, deeply ingrained in the psyche of the Muslims worldwide. It always had and continues to have an aura of special respect and sanctity in the eyes of the faithful.

The high regard for the traditional Caliphate in the hearts of Muslims worldwide has been capitalized upon by Abu Bakr al-Baghdadi. Under his charismatic leadership ISIS has become the world's most successful terrorist group, financially secure and militarily quite powerful. It must be admitted that Baghdadi has managed to propel the Caliphate to the world stage seemingly out of nowhere, by sheer savagery, including the beheadings on camera of several American hostages. He has been trying to overawe the world by overrunning international borders in the Middle East, Libya, Nigeria, Somalia, Afghanistan and many other Muslim-dominated regions. In India too, the Kashmir valley has witnessed regular waving of the black flags of ISIS during Friday prayers.

After defeating his opponents, Al-Baghdadi carved out a radical State which rules over nearly nine million people and has captured large swathes of territories which are larger in size than the United Kingdom. By carrying out the genocide of non-Muslims, ISIS managed to expand the lure of Islamic glory in many Muslim countries like Libya, Tunisia, Nigeria, and Caucasus in Russia. Islamic State has occupied the mindscape of Muslims in Indonesia and even in the faraway Mindnao and Sulu groups of islands in southern Philippines.

The blood-drenched narrative of the newly created Caliphate and its military conquests is an amazing success story. The Islamic State has a conquest-oriented religion – it is called the religion of the sword. It rules over an expansive territory in West Asia and parts of Africa in accordance with the Takfiri ideology which has deep roots in the psyche of Muslims worldwide. Takfiris are an ultra violent offshoot of the Salafi movement. They openly preach murder and mayhem and condone acts of violence in pursuit of Islam's religious and political goals. They believe that Islam must be practiced strictly in accordance with the interpretation of Prophet Muhammad's actions and the traditions established by him and his companions. As pointed out by Robert Baer, a well-known expert on the Middle East, Takfiris are Sunni Muslim whose mission is to create a global caliphate as envisaged in the Qur'an and enforce the Sharia. Al-Baghdadi has revived the longing of the faithful to restore the long lost grandeur of Islam.

Savagery Used as Force-Multiplier

A critical study of the history of Islamic wars waged in India and across several other countries during medieval times and modern era reveals the ugly contours of relentless use of savagery against the Hindus of India and Christians of the Balkans and Spain. Unfortunately many analysts and security experts have failed to understand that during medieval times 'savagery' was used as a powerful "force- multiplier" by the Muslim invaders and rulers. It was the single most important reason for the dramatic victories of Islam worldwide. The same strategy of ruthless savagery has been adopted by ISIS in their campaigns in Syria, Iraq, Levant and parts of Africa. The strategy has been borrowed from the scriptural narratives followed by Islamic warriors throughout history, and further honed by Abu Bakr Naji who is the real ideologue of Islamic State. Recourse to widespread savagery to terrorize non-Muslims during jihad has been advocated by Naji in his tome, '*Management of Savagery*'. The scriptural guidelines prescribed by Naji are being implemented in the Caliphate controlled by al-Baghdadi for imposing Sharia and capturing more territory. Large scale beheadings of kaffirs and abduction of Yazidi and Christian women for sex-slavery are two prominent examples of the savagery unleashed by the storm-troopers of the Caliphate. In scale and methodology their tactics are totally comparable to the barbarism practiced in India by Islamic invaders. A similar strategy for seeking victory over the Christian kaffirs was successfully replicated by Ottoman Turks in Eastern Europe.

Islam's Umbilical Connection with Savagery

In a seminally researched article titled, 'Death By Fire Is An Islamic Punishment', Yasmin Al Khatib, an Egyptian author, wrote that the people who claim that the "ISIS brutality has nothing to do with Islam" are liars.[1] She has highlighted the fact that the entire Muslim history – including the history of the Prophet and his followers – is rife with stories of grisly executions and beheadings, which show that such actions are not foreign to Islam. Reproduced below are some very informative excerpts from her remarkably frank article:

> "I do not understand why, after every perverted act of execution carried out by ISIS, most Muslims (and Western leaders) insist that these actions have nothing to do with Islam. After all, Muslim history is rife with terrifying forms of execution, similar or even identical to those used by ISIS."[2]

Yasmin draws attention to the methods of execution used during the early Islamic period, a period which most Muslim clerics regard as the source of Islamic legislation and victories, such as execution by fire, or by being flung from a high place – the two specific punishments prescribed for homosexuals. The consensus among the Prophet's companions was that all homosexuals should be put to death, but they disagreed on the method. Some thought that a homosexual should be burned alive, others advocated toppling a wall over him and leaving him to die under the rubble, and yet others thought he should be thrown from the highest wall in the village and then pelted with stones until he died. The last method was applied by ISIS to a homosexual who was cast from a tall building in Baghdad. The first and fourth Caliphs, Abu Bakr and Ali bin-Abu Talib, had ordered the burning alive of homosexuals, and this was often done. Abu Bakr was a learned companion and father-in-law of Prophet Muhammad.

Yasmin in her critical article points out that a book by the Islamic scholar Al-Tabari states that during the hey days of Islam, Caliph Abu Bakr had ordered his commanders, waging wars against the apostates, to burn several of them, and the book *Futuh al-Buldan* (*Conquest of Lands*) expressly states that the Muslim military leader and companion of the Prophet, Khaled bin Al-Walid, also burned some apostate hostages. These examples demonstrate that Islamic thought is not totally free of responsibility for the notion of execution by fire – a fact that some people ignored, either deliberately or out of ignorance, argues the bold scholar. Indeed, the execution by fire of the Jordanian pilot Mu'adh Al-Kassasbeh was carried out by the ISIS in the first week of February 2015, as per Islamic tradition.

These people justified their position by quoting the hadith of the Prophet – 'none is permitted to torture by fire but the Master of fire, i.e., Allah, even though this command starkly contradicts the accounts of the Prophet's companions executing people by fire. Yasmin Khatib admits that she herself was inclined to question this hadith, since it first orders to burn people and then says the opposite. According to her the full text of the hadith proclaims thus:

> *The Prophet dispatched a squadron of warriors, telling them: "If you find the man named so-and-so and the man named so-and-so, burn them both in fire."*

Later on the Prophet said that he had given orders to burn those two men in the fire, but none is permitted to torture by fire but the Master of fire (Allah). So he ordered that they shall be killed. In any case, the Umayyad Caliphs continued meting out the punishment of death by fire, and later the Abbasid Caliphs even improved upon it – by roasting the condemned man over a slow fire until he expired, just like you would roast a slaughtered animal, according to Yasmin Khatib.

As for torturing people to death, the aforesaid scholar referred to the well-known episode about the men of Urayna in Arabia who had seized Prophet's camels. The man who was tending them had been killed, after gouging out his eyes with a sharp sword, cutting off his arms, legs and tongue, and then left him to die. When the Prophet heard of this, he ordered his followers to cut off the arms and legs of the transgressors, gouge out their eyes with a red-hot iron and then cast them out into the streets until they died. This punishment was in accordance with the Islamic principle of subjecting the perpetrator to whatever they did to others.

Yasmin admits that Christianity, too, had a very violent history. But somehow, Christianity changed over the years by choosing the path of enlightenment. Islam must do the same, she argues. Otherwise thousands of Islamic organizations like ISIS will emerge. She further emphasizes that enlightenment is the only weapon for defeating ISIS. The real war is not against ISIS but against extremist Islamic thinking, and if we do not confront it, a thousand other ISIS-type Islamic groups will emerge.

While concluding her thesis on Islamic savagery she advises liberal intellectuals to tell Muslims, when the latter advise them to read the Quran to understand why the savagery of ISIS is un-Islamic, to show them her analysis and videos depicting savagery, to prove that "ISIS brutality is as Islamic as you can get."

Yasmin Khatib challenges the assertions made by Barack Obama, David Cameron, Council on American-Islamic Relations CAIR), and the Sharia-compliant media who keep insisting that ISIS has nothing to do with Islam. The lady scholar's indictment of the likes of Obama and Cameron for denying the truth applies equally well to the hordes of sham-secularist intellectuals and tele-media analysts of India who keep trotting out that terrorists have no religion. The key role played by terror and savagery in winning the Holy Wars has been candidly admitted in Sahi Bukhari 4.52.220. It claims that Prophet Muhammad had candidly proclaimed, "I have been made victorious by recourse to terror".

Yasmin Khatib Endorsed

Similar views about the connection between savagery and Islam were expressed by an Egyptian Television host Ibrahim Issa, on February 3, 2015.[3] He pointed out that whenever ISIS carried out an act of barbarity, such as decapitation, throat slitting, or burning alive of a person, various Sheikhs would tell us that this had nothing to do with Islam and that Islam was not to blame. But ISIS soldiers committing slaughter, rape and immolation openly claim that they are motivated by Sharia and Islamic scriptures. He made bold to state that "all the evidence and references that ISIS provides, claiming that they can be found in the books of history, jurisprudence and law, are indeed, to be found there, and anyone who says otherwise is lying."[4]

Savagery Creates Caliphate

The ideologue of Islamic State, Abu Bakr Naji, himself has admitted that "the administration of savagery has been established in Islamic history various times". He recalls that *the first example of savagery was the establishment of the Islamic state in Medina*[5] The following quote from Naji's war manual, *Management of Savagery*, shows the importance which the Caliph and his storm-troopers attach to using savagery as a force-multiplier for achieving victory in West Asia and across the globe.

> *"One can consider the era prior to the first stage of the Medinan era – before it was stable and established as a state to which zakat and jizya were given and before it became permanent receiving the recognition of the provinces around it and appointing governors and rulers – at the time when Medina was administered according to the order of the*

administration of savagery. Of course Medina was not suffering from savagery before the hijra of the Prophet (Peace be upon Him); but it was administered by tribes like the Aws and Khazraj with an order that resembled the order of the administration of savagery. When Muhammad (Peace be upon Him) emigrated to Medina with a similar order (to that of the Aws and Khazraj); it was an ideal order for administration of savagery, whose features we set forth above." [6]

It may be mentioned that Banū Aws and Khazraj were two ancient tribes of Arabia in the pre-Islamic era. The two communities constituted the Ansars (i.e., "the helpers" of Prophet Muhammad) after his Hijrat to Medina.

In the 21st Century, savagery has been used, once again, as a force-multiplier by Muslims to establish a Caliphate in West Asia. According to Abu Bakr Naji the ideologue of the ISIS, "the administration of savagery has been established in our Islamic history various times".

For strategizing a plan to defeat the challenge of Al-Baghdadi's storm-troopers it is important to understand that during medieval times 'savagery' was used as a force multiplier by the soldiers of Islam.

Not many strategic analysts know that Abu Bakr Naji is the ideologue of Al-Baghdadi's Caliphate and that his infamous book, *Management of Savagery*, has become the guiding principle of the Islamic Caliphate. The book was published online in 2004. It was translated into English in the year 2006 by William Mc Cants, who is a Fellow at the *West Point Combating Terror Center*. The English translation was funded by John M. Olin Institute for Strategic Studies at Harvard University. Not much is known about the background of

Abu Bakr Naji, apart from the fact that he has been a frequent contributor to the al-Qaeda's mouthpiece, a magazine titled *"The Voice of Jihad"*. According to the Al Arabiya Institute for Islamic Studies, the real identity of Abu Bakr Naji is Muhammad Khalil al-Hakaymah. His known works are this remarkable treatise on using savagery as a war-winning strategy, apart from his contributions made to al-Qaeda's online magazine *Sawt al-Jihad*, which means *"Lovers of Paradise"*. The said online journal is a professional guide for training the jihadi recruits.

By taking a page out of the writings of the famous Islamic theologian, Ibn Taymiyya of Sham (Syria), Naji has been advocating the use of raw savagery to terrorize and defeat kaffirs. Originally Abu Bakr Naji penned a strategic treatise titled, *Idārat at-Tawahhush: Akhtar marhalah satamourrou biha al ummah*) which reads like a war manual. Translated into English, the title of the book means *Management of Savagery*.

The core emphasis of Naji's thesis is on creating pockets of vexation and political exhaustion by unleashing unremitting savagery for acquiring control of the selected target areas. He calls it a strategic prelude to the birth of an Islamic state. An important aspect of Naji's vision is a belief in recourse to barbaric killings in the battlefield for educating and training new jihadi cadres. While listing the key requirements for ''managing savagery'' in areas where jihadists gain territorial control, he specifically emphasizes the need to raise the level of self-belief and combat efficiency during training of the youth in the use of savagery to establish a fighting Islamic society at all levels.

Unlike many apologists for Islam, including the American President, Barack Obama, the soldiers of the Islamic State don't lie; won't lie. They proudly proclaim that they are doing what has been sanctioned by the Prophet himself in Islamic scriptures.

Naji's Formula for Victory of Islam

According to Naji, for establishing an Islamic State, the Ummah, i.e., the Muslims, will have to walk through the following three stages.

- The first stage will be to increase the power of "vexation and exhaustion" in pockets located in the targeted areas of the selected country.
- The second stage will comprise the stepping up of the administration of savagery by jihadi groups to create chaos and lawlessness.
- And thereafter will come the third stage, namely the moment of victory after acquiring the power of establishing the Islamic state.

A close study of the resounding success of Al-Baghdadi's Caliphate in Syria, Iraq, Levant and parts of African continent reveals how by recourse to gross savagery the above mentioned three stages have been accomplished.

The 'pockets of vexation and exhaustion' advocated by Naji are nothing but the areas widely perceived and called in common parlance as "no-go zones" created by radical Muslims in several cities of various countries, including India. These are the areas where the law-enforcers remain frequently locked in conflict with organized gangs of determined mobsters. In these Muslim-dominated ghettoes, the rowdies don't allow non-Muslims to enter their turf. Examples of pockets of 'vexation and exhaustion' created by radical Muslims in the world are many, including the Chechnya region of Russia, the tribal areas of Afghanistan and AFPAK region. India, too, is dotted with scores of pockets of 'vexation and exhaustion' in the Kashmir Valley, western Uttar Pradesh, Kerala, Karnataka and West Bengal, where entry of security forces is opposed by Islamic militants and saboteurs. Other prominent examples are the multiple zones of battle with kaffirs (read the Christians) in Nigeria, Libya, Somalia and Mali. These areas have been captured by Boko Haram and Al Shabab, the two violent outfits which have declared themselves as Affiliates of the ISIS. The militancy in the southern States of Thailand and the holy war being waged by the militants of Moro Islamic Liberation Front in southern Philippines (Mindnao and Sulu Islands), too, are prominent pockets of vexation and exhaustion. There are hundreds of no-go zones all over Europe. In a broad sense all Muslim-dominated areas, whether in Europe, or in India, can be converted into 'pockets of vexation and exhaustion' by ensuring that the police and non-Muslims are not allowed to enter without facing resistance.

Battlefield as Best Training Ground

In Naji's scheme of things, the ideal of education by example (i.e., *tarbiya bil-qudwa*) is one of the two most effective methods of training the Mujahideen. He devotes a great deal of space to elaborating on this method by emphasizing that seeing someone sacrifice things which he most values, in the path of Allah, will have a strong inspirational effect on the beholders. The examples of the strategy used by Prophet and his companions were their dazzling exploits, which acted as exemplars for the masses. When there are men in the ranks of Mujtahids who sacrifice expensive and valuable things in response to Allah's commands they are bound to become the best means of educating the believers in Islamic activism and for motivating young jihadis. *Prima facie* ''martyrdom'' or suicide operations carried out by Islamic militants fall in this category.

The second important aspect of jihadi training is imparting education by staging "momentous events'' or spectacular attacks (called *tarbiya bil-ahadath*). Naji has emphasized the importance of staging 'spectacular attacks' on the enemy. He recommends that while using the strategy of savagery, it is necessary to stage momentous events to motivate Islamic warriors. According to him the method of staging momentous events is the most effective means for attracting the youth to ISIS. He reiterates that "terrible events" (i.e., spectacular strikes against infidels) which capture the imagination of the people, will have a greater learning effect than a hundred years of peaceful education. Such "momentous events" tend to produce Islamic heroes and demonstrate the resolve of jihadi warriors to win in the face of the horrors of war. The attack on twin towers and Pentagon on 11th September, 2001, was a typical example of a 'momentous event' (*tarbiya bil-ahadath*). Similarly the December, 2001 attack on Indian Parliament and the Mumbai massacre of 26th November, 2008, by ten Pakistani Fedayeen's were two more example of 'momentous events', or spectacular attacks. The recent attacks in America, France, Belgium and Bangladesh, et. al., are striking examples of '*tarbiya bil-ahadath*', or spectacular attacks on kaffirs.

Naji's action-oriented educational program appears to be somewhat dismissive of the traditional methods of merely reciting the Holy Quran or teaching the Islamic laws and imparting moral lessons there from. For Naji, the real jihadi training and education can be truly effective only during action and in the battlefield. Therefore, the Islamic warriors should be taught and trained in savagery on battleground during action while executing military operations. They should subject the enemy to savagery and also make bold to face the savage attacks unleashed on them.

The self-appointed caliph Al-Baghdadi has implemented the guidelines enunciated in Abu Bakr Naji's tome, *Management of Savagery*. A number of barbaric practices have been borrowed from Islamic scriptures and narratives of victories scored by Muslim freebooters in medieval times. The soldiers of ISIS have also been destroying all monuments dating to the pre-Islamic era in the same manner in which Muslim armies had destroyed Hindu temples across India and Christian churches in Europe in the not too distant past.

Apparently not many Indian strategic analysts and tele-anchors have cared to study the vicious book, *Management of Savagery*. Some of them might not even know that Abu Bakr Naji is the ideologue of Al-Baghdadi's Caliphate and that his infamous book is being used as the war manual by ISIS. In essence the strategic construct of limitless savagery against kaffirs, practiced in the medieval era, continues to rule the hearts and minds of Al-Baghdadi and his storm-troopers.

To recapitulate, by turning to the scriptural sanction for terrorizing the kaffirs and by replicating the strategy employed during global campaigns in the medieval times, savagery has been used as the most lethal weapon of Al-Baghdadi's holy war. The soldiers of ISIS have been trained to be brutal - for beheading, maiming, enslaving and ruthlessly murdering the non-Muslims.

Decoding Islamic State

Islamic State is no longer a mere theoretical idea. It is alive and kicking and has grown far more powerful than any other Islamic group across the globe. It is a politically-charged military concept aimed at imposing the ultra-orthodox Islamic ideology on all non-Muslim countries by force. Equally remarkable is the fact that their affiliate groups have been hyperactive in parts of Nigeria, Somalia, Libya, Tunisia, Mali and other parts of North Africa – even in the Caucasus region of Russia and faraway Brazil. The territory captured by the ISIS in West Asia is presently governed from Raqqa in Syria. The group claims that they are merely practicing true Islam by using the Salafi principles for wholesale slaughter of the kaffirs opposing the supremacy of Islam.

Originally Islamic State had grown out of an outfit called Jamaat al - Tahwid Wal-Jihad (JTWJ). It was founded in 1999 by Abu Musab al-Zarqawi. Initially the group focused on attempting a regime change in Jordan. Zarqawi had gained experience as a jihadi warrior first in

Afghanistan and had met Osama Bin Laden in 1999. His views differed substantially from Laden's approach about the mode of waging global jihad. Unlike Laden, Zarqawi came from a poor family and had a more aggressive and violent temperament.

Immediately after the invasion of Iraq by the United States in 2003 Zarqawi raised the banner of revolt against the American forces. An important feature of his personality was a pronounced proclivity towards ferocious brutality while battling the enemy. His hatred for Shias was enormous and he used to refer to them as lurking snakes. Gradually his pronounced hatred for Shias became an integral component of the ISIS ideology.

A high profile terrorist attack organized by Jamat-al Tawhid Wal-Jihad was the one launched in August, 2003, on the UN compound in Baghdad in which twenty two persons, including the Special Representative of United Nations, were killed. Again in February 2004 during the Ashura festival the outfit killed 150 Shias in simultaneous attacks in Baghdad and across Karbala, the holiest Shia city. Zarqawi further earned great notoriety by personally carrying out the beheadings of two American hostages, Eugene Armstrong and Jack Hensley in September, 2004.

Ultimately Zarqawi joined hands with Al Qaeda and re-named his group - Al-Qaeda in the Land of the Two Rivers (Tigris and the Euphrates). It was also called as Al-Qaeda in Iraq, or AQI. Within two years, around 2006, Zarqawi's outfit morphed into an autonomous entity. He started his own ultra violent campaign of jihad and gathered several Iraqi factions under the banner of the Majlis-e-Shura al-Mujahedin (MSM). He focused more on developing the basic infrastructure needed for enforcing the Sharia law which was the group's goal. Zarqawi was killed in 2006 by the US forces in an airstrike targeting him. After his death the group was led by Abu Ayyub Al-Masri and thereafter by Abu Omar al-Baghdadi, both of whom were killed in 2010. Earlier in 2006, the group had again changed its name to the Islamic State in Iraq (ISI). Their prime intention was to conquer a part of Iraq for creating a Sharia – compliant State there. Thereafter they started working on capturing large swathes of territory in the desert region of Anbar province of Iraq where discontent among the Sunni population was at a high pitch.

In 2010, the present caliph, Abu Bakr al-Baghdadi, took over the Islamic State of Iraq. He succeeded in rebuilding substantial popular support by regenerating the organization. Al-Baghdadi has a long history of waging jihad. Originally he belonged to the terrorist brigade of Al-Qaeda and had been arrested by the Americans in 2003. After serving his prison term he was released in 2009 and re-emerged as a powerful Islamic leader during the Syrian Civil War in 2013. Once again he renamed the organization as the Islamic State in Iraq and Syria (or the Islamic State in Iraq, Syria and Levant, i.e., ISIL). Al-Baghdadi's decision to move into Syria provoked a minor fight with the Al-Qaeda's official affiliate in Syria, a group known as Jabhat-al Nusra. But Al-Baghdadi's attempt to take over Jabhat al-Nusra failed. The two opposing groups, the ISIS and Al Nusra, differed in their approach for establishing the Caliphate. Al Nusra wanted to follow a more gradual approach for establishing a Caliphate. On the contrary, Al-Baghdadi favored the strategy of capitalizing on the momentum by seizing more territories for carving out an Islamic State at the earliest and enforcing Sharia.

During 2013 and in early 2014 the ISIS kept on building a powerful base in Syria by establishing its stronghold in the famous town of Raqqa, which it was able to seize after an inconsequential battle. The ISIS fully subscribes to the Takfiri ideology of Islam which is also the ideology of the rulers of Saudi Arabia. For that reason there is a lurking suspicion that many Sheikhs of Saudi Arabia and Middle East are sympathetic to the cause espoused by Islamic State. Ultimately ISIS was able to consolidate its power base in Syria and Iraq. At the same time, the group never forgot the importance of capturing Iraq – a vital step forward, in furtherance of their campaign. In January 2014, their soldiers captured parts of Falluja and Ramadi in Anbar province. Soon thereafter in early June, 2014, Islamic State shocked the Americans by capturing Mosul which is Iraq's second largest city. Finally on June 29, 2014, the first day of the holy month of Ramadan, ISIS declared the establishment of the Caliphate. Abu Bakr al-Baghdadi proclaimed himself as Caliph Ibrahim and gave a call for the total loyalty and obedience of all Muslims in the world. In January, 2015, the group declared the city of Falluja a part of the Islamic State.

In Islamic folklore the Caliph is an incredibly important religious figure and the re-establishment of the Caliphate has been a long standing goal of all Islamic and jihadi groups, right from the Muslim Brotherhood in Egypt to Jamaat-e-Islami functioning in Pakistan and India. To comprehend the theological importance of Caliph one has to recall to mind the religious fervour displayed by Indian Muslims during the notorious Khilafat movement of 1920s. Supported by Gandhiji they wanted continuation of the Ottoman caliphate. Spiritually speaking, the Caliph is deemed to be the successor to the founder of Islam, Prophet Mohammed. In order to increase his legitimacy as a global Muslim leader, Abu Bakr al-Baghdadi, claimed descent from Prophet Mohammed and has been using the surname 'al-Qureshi'. Among Muslims the Prophet's clan, Quraish, has huge status value.

The Caliphate was the original form of government established by the successors of Prophet Mohammed to govern the countries under Islamic rule. The first four Caliphs, called the Rashidun (the rightly-guided), oversaw the rapid expansion of Muslim dominions from its starting point in Saudi Arabia to one of the historically largest empires in the world. The Caliphate is therefore highly romanticized by jihadis, as it harkens back to an era when the Islamic empire was rapidly expanding and came to be recognized as the most powerful force. A few community leaders and leading lights of Islamic groups, including some Indian Ulemas, have rejected the claim of Islamic State to be recognized as a Caliphate. Their plea that it does not meet the religious preconditions required to be accepted as a valid Caliphate made no impact in the Islamic world. Consequently the long march of the ISIS continues unchallenged and unabated.

Though Zarqawi was killed on June 7, 2006, by the US Air Force, his ideology continues to rule the hearts of the Sunni militants of Iraq, Syria and several African countries. Several thousand Muslims have gone from Western countries to join the Islamic State. This is an unprecedented development which has never been seen before for any other Islamic group. Samuel Oakford of the *Soufan Group*, a New York based terrorism tracking consultancy, places the total number of foreigners from various countries fighting in Syria and Iraq between 20,000 and 31, 000.[7]

According to informed researchers as many as 31,000 people from at least 86 countries have travelled to Syria and Iraq to fight for the Islamic State and other extremist groups since 2011. In a new report the Soufan group said the number of new recruits have roughly doubled from an earlier assessment made in the summer of 2014. Though the latest numbers largely confirm the earlier estimates made by the US and the United Nations, the data provides more detailed accounts of the countries and regions from which thousands of fighters have emerged. Roughly half of the foreign fighters hail from the Middle East and North Africa. Battle – hardened Jihadi militants from Tunisia, who may number as many as 7,000, continue to have an outsized presence among the fighters in Iraq and Syria. In a country of less than 11 million people, such a large figure is an important concern for the Tunisian officials.

In an interview with the VICE News, Patrick Skinner, Director of Special Projects at the Soufan Group said that the influx of foreigners into West Asia started to peak at the end of last year, following the blitzkrieg expansion of ISIS in northern Iraq. It exploded in the fall and winter, said Skinner. It may be pointed out that due to limited reporting, it is difficult to know the exact number of jihadists joining ISIS. But the Soufan group's tabulations, like the figure of 30,000 arrived at by US intelligence officials, is likely to include fighters who were killed or returned home. In June, 2015, the officials of the State Department of America estimated that nearly 10,000 ISIS fighters, both local and foreign, had been killed since the start of the US-led airstrikes in 2014.

ISIS Affiliates Worldwide

The ISIS is well-known for having caught the fancy of the Muslims around the world. It has established a network of Military Affiliates in many countries across the world to support the ISIS. Several Affiliates are believed to have thousands of members.[8] Beyond the low-stake demonstrations of popular sympathy for ISIS, more than a dozen militant organizations in several countries (in addition to Iraq and Syria) have made formal pledges of support to the group, making these outfits, in a real sense, part of the fighting force of the Islamic State. ISIS has been designating these Military Affiliates as 'Wilayats' which means a province of Islamic State. For all practical purposes the Wilayats are required to function as foreign bases of Islamic State. They are operating as outposts of ISIS for waging jihad.

The well-known analyst, Veryan Khan, who is Editorial Director of the Terrorism Research & Analysis Consortium (TRAC), explained the process to the Intelligencer team. Support for ISIS among other radical groups, she said, is manifesting in one or more of three ways:

At the basic level, members of Islamic groups tend to show support for the ISIS ideology by sporting the group's flags and logo. Then there are groups that are more committed and pledge loyalty to ISIS as a symbolic statement. The most committed groups, however, make a formal declaration of bay'ah, or allegiance, to the Islamic State, and become official allies or affiliates. In the history of Islam such pledges were given to Caliphs by the nations submitting to Islam. What shape, exactly, these alliances take can vary, in part depending on the distance between Baghdadi and the central leadership of the group, or Wilayat.

The Terrorism Research & Analysis Consortium (TRAC) has identified a number of groups located outside Iraq and Syria who have made a formal pledge of allegiance to ISIS and Baghdadi. There may be many more who have done so without publicizing their agreements. While some of them are large established groups, others are comparatively new and unknown. In most cases, the precise membership numbers are not available. Given below is a country-by-country look at the expanding network of partners and affiliated groups of Islamic State.

1. Pakistan

Though local authorities in Pakistan keep on insisting that ISIS has no presence in Pakistan, the reality on the ground is altogether different. ISIS is very much rooted in Pakistani soil and has established collaborative ties with Hafiz Saeed of Jamaat-ud-Dawa and Jaish-e-Muhammad. The agents and activists of ISIS are reported to be in touch with many other militant groups, too. Pledges of allegiance to the Islamic State by a section of the Taliban have also been reported. In fact, a group of former Taliban militants from Pakistan and Afghanistan had filmed themselves beheading a captive in the name of ISIS in the year 2015. Meanwhile, it has been highlighted by the

New York Times and several news agencies that lately the black standard of the Islamic State has been popping up all over Pakistan.

Recently a Taliban splinter group Jundallah joined a handful of other Tehrik-i-Taliban Pakistan affiliates who have already pledged allegiance to ISIS. They claimed that ISIS warriors were their brothers and whatever plan they have chalked out, Jundallah will support them in it. The Taliban leadership has historic ties with the central Al Qaeda leaders. Therefore, a pledge of allegiance to ISIS is a strong signal that Al Qaeda is losing support in Pakistan. Meanwhile ISIS has gained support from Pakistani militants like Tehreek-e-Khilafat – a Taliban-linked group that became the first Pakistani supporter of ISIS in July 2015. The members of Jamaat *al-Ahrar*, a significant group which had split from the Tehreek-Taliban-Pakistan in August, 2014, too, are reported to be aligned with Islamic State. The Islamic State confirmed its presence in Pakistan by staging two spectacular attacks. First, there was an attack in Lahore on the Christians celebrating Easter in the last week of March, 2016. It was followed by an attack on lawyers in Quetta (Balochistan) on 8 August, 2016, in which 70 persons were killed.

2. Egypt

Islamic terrorist groups are particularly active in Egypt's lawless Sinai Peninsula. The most well-known of them is Wilayat Sinai or Ansar Beit al-Maqdis. The group pledged allegiance to the ISIS in November, 2014, hoping that the partnership will provide them with more resources and weapons. The radical group, initially known as Ansar Beit al-Maqdis (Supporters of House of Jerusalem), has been active in the Sinai Peninsula since 2012. It changed its name to Sinai Province, or Wilayat Sinai, after pledging allegiance to Islamic State. The soldiers of Wilayat Sinai were successful in staging multiple attacks against the Egyptian army in the year 2015. The strength of its soldiers is believed to be around 1,500 or more. The group is reported to have carried out more than two dozen attacks across Sinai within a span of less than three weeks in March, 2016. A video released in the third week of January, 2016, on the occasion of the fifth anniversary of the 2011 revolution, called upon its supporters to step up their fight against the Egyptian President Abdul Al-Sisi. The jihadi group Wilayat Sinai, has been linked to a number of deadly attacks in North Sinai as well as in Cairo.

3. Algeria

Like many Pakistani groups, the Algeria-based Soldiers of the Caliphate, also known as Jund al-Khilafa, had ties with central Al Qaeda leaders like Osama bin Laden and Ayman al-Zawahiri. The Soldiers were a splinter group of Al Qaeda in the Islamic Maghreb and formally pledged allegiance to ISIS. Their leader Gouri Abdelmalek, a.k.a. Khaled Abu Suleimane, claimed in a statement that Al Qaeda and allied groups had deviated from the true path due to which his group was aligning with Islamic State. Less than two weeks after pledging allegiance, the Soldiers of Caliphate beheaded a French citizen Hervé Gourdel after France participated in airstrikes on ISIS in Iraq.

4. Libya

A relatively new and unknown group of radicals took over the coastal Libyan city of Derna in April, 2014. The organization, which calls itself the Islamic Youth Shura Council (IYSC), was founded in that city. Like many Islamic groups, initially it had allied itself with Al Qaeda, but quickly switched allegiance to Islamic State. In October, 2014, the Islamic Youth Shura Council declared that Derna was now an outpost of the ISIS known as Wilayat Derna. This is one of the few ISIS outposts that actually controls a large part of the coastal area of

Libya. It is feared that the group's influence may spread across inland because of the ongoing political instability.

The best success of ISIS was the capture of Sirte in February, 2015, which is another important city on Libya's Mediterranean coast. The Islamic State claimed it as its first territory, outside of Syria and Iraq. According to the estimates of Libyan intelligence, the ISIS presence there has grown from 200 committed fighters a year ago, to a roughly 5,000 – strong contingent which includes administrators and financiers.

Libya has a strong ISIS presence. The country's neighbours have become increasingly alarmed. Tunisia closed its border with Libya for 15 days in November, 2015, after Islamic State claimed responsibility for a bomb blast in a bus in its capital Tunis that killed 12 presidential guards. Tunisia is also building a security wall along a third of that border to stem the inflow of extremists from Libya. Two previous attacks in 2015 had killed dozens of tourists visiting Tunisia. These were carried out by gunmen trained by Islamic State in Libya.

In Libya, Islamic State has called for recruits having technical knowhow to put nearby oil facilities into operation. Libyan officials are worried because it is only a matter of time before the radical fighters take over more oil fields and refineries near Sirte to boost their revenues. That will generate more revenue to fund attacks in the Middle East and Europe. Sirte is the gateway to several major oil fields and refineries farther east on the same coast and the Islamic State has targeted those installations in the past years. "They have made their intentions clear," said Ismail Shoukry, head of Libyan government's military intelligence for the region that includes Sirte. They want to take their fight to Rome, Shoukry asserted.[9] But recently in a major setback to ISIS the pro-government Libyan troops have managed to wrest control of Sirte from the radical group affiliated to Islamic State. It is a major loss in Libya for Islamic State.

5. The Philippines

The radical group led by Abu Sayyaf has become an associate of ISIS in the Philippines. He is a committed jihadi and leader of the Moro Islamic Liberation Front (M.I.L.F). The group led by him is based in the Sulu and Mindnao Islands of southern Philippines. It is dedicated to carving out an Islamic state in the country and has pledged allegiance to Al-Baghdadi. In its past history it had ties with Al Qaeda. The group had once kidnapped two German hostages whom they threatened to behead if Germany didn't pay a ransom. The pair was later released reportedly after the militants received about $5 million in ransom. But in April, 2016 the group beheaded, a Canadian national whom they had captured in September, 2015, because the ransom money was not paid.

6. Ansar Beit al-Maqdis in Gaza

The Gaza-based *Ansar Beit al-Maqdis* group has been discussed in the Egypt section. It has changed its name to Sinai Province or Wilayat Sinai. It has pledged allegiance to the Islamic State. The outfit has assembled an army of nearly 1,500 soldiers and is reported to be growing in strength. It is also known as Al-Dawla al-Islamiyya, which means Islamic State. The organization is believed to have fired some rockets into Israel.

7. Lebanon

In Lebanon the 'Free Sunnis of Baalbek Brigade' is a militant group fighting against the Shia influence. It has been engaged in a violent struggle against Shia outfits. The outfit also took responsibility for the 2013 bombing of the Iranian embassy in Beirut. It gave bay'ah, or an oath of allegiance, to ISIS in the year 2014.

8. Indonesia

Abu Bakar Bashir, the incarcerated leader of the Java-based Ashor-ut Tauhid movement, pledged allegiance to ISIS from his jail cell in July, 2014. Bashir is serving a 15-year sentence for running a jihadi training camp in Indonesia. The group broke off from a larger terror organization known as Jemaah Islamiyah and has taken responsibility for the church bombings in Indonesia. The multiple terror attacks in Jakarta on 14th January, 2016, confirmed that ISIS is powerfully entrenched in Indonesia.

9. Jordan

A youth militant movement called Sons of the Call for Tawhid and Jihad is ISIS's main affiliate in Jordan. The group started out as a branch of the country's Salafist movement and now constitutes the majority of its members. It denounced Al Qaeda leaders in July, 2014 and declared that it was their right and duty to join Islamic State.

10. Afghanistan

In recent times ISIS has made substantial territorial gains in Afghanistan, including the infamous Tora Bora region. The development has forced the United States to significantly increase its aerial bombing campaign.[10] The Afghan and American commanders admit that currently, the presence of the Taliban appears stronger than at any point since 2001. They have nearly 20,000 to 40,000 fighters and their estimated strength is said to be far greater than the number of militants aligned with Islamic State. The real danger to peace in Afghanistan, howsoever, comes from the Taliban soldiers shifting their loyalty to Islamic State. Many Islamic State fighters operating in the country happen to be former members of the Pakistani Taliban. The message sent by the 27th March, 2016, attack on the Easter crowd in Lahore by Jamaat-ul-Ahrar (a former faction of Tehrik-e-Taliban Pakistan now supposedly aligned with ISIS) must not be ignored. A notorious militant outfit of Taliban led by Hafeez Saeed Khan, has become the tenth military affiliate of the Islamic State. He, along with thirty other senior Taliban leaders, has defected to ISIS. Meanwhile the popularity and strength of ISIS in Afghanistan has been growing rapidly. It is a relatively new force in Afghanistan and there are contradictory assessments about its actual strength. No one knows that how strong it is and how closely it is operationally linked with the main arm in Iraq and Syria. Security experts say that many members of ISIS in Afghanistan happen to be former Taliban fighters who fell out with the current leadership. Some of them were those who wanted a more extreme form of militant activity to be pursued. The lone-wolf attack mounted by the ISIS on Pakistan's Consulate in Jalalabad in Nangarhar Province in the second week of January, 2016, demonstrated the growth of the jihadi cult of Islamic State in Afghanistan.

11. Nigeria

The militant Islamic outfit Boko Haram which has been spearheading a bloody campaign across Nigeria, targeting Christians and their churches, declared allegiance to Islamic State in March, 2015. Previously it was affiliated to Al Qaeda. The ultraviolent group is based in northeastern Nigeria and is also known as *Wilāyat Gharb Ifrīqīyyah* (Islamic State of West Africa Province, *ISWAP*). This radical outfit is also active in Chad, Niger and northern Cameroon. During the last seven years it has killed nearly 20,000 innocents and displaced approximately 2.3 million people from their homes. In April, 2014, it had abducted 276 non-Muslim school girls from Chibok. In the middle of 2014 the militants belonging to the outfit had taken control of nearly 50 thousand square kilometers area in and around the Bono State of Nigeria. But they could not capture the state capital, Maiduguri despite persistent efforts. The outfit is notorious for committing human rights abuses and is violently opposed to western education and Christians. It was ranked as the world's deadliest terror group in the year 2015, according to the Global Terrorism Index.

12. Somalia

In the last week of October, 2015, the dangerously violent Islamic terrorist organization Al Shabab, with its headquarters in Somalia, also declared allegiance to Islamic State, after which it has stepped up its violent activities in Somalia and adjoining countries.

13. Mali

There was an attack on Radisson Hotel Blu' in Bamako (Mali) on 15 November, 2015, in which 20 foreigners were killed. The media blamed Al Qaeda for the killings. There is a strong possibility of the attack being engineered by ISIS which is now firmly entrenched in western Africa. A significant clue to the complicity of the Islamic State is the fact that the attack in Bamako took place barely one week after the November, 2015, Paris attack which claimed 130 lives.

14. Burkina Faso

A spectacular attack was launched on 15th January, 2016, in Ouagadougou the capital of Burkina Faso. It was carried out by the ISIS Fedayeen's who stormed the Splendid Hotel where foreign nationals prefer to stay. The two countries, Burkina Faso and Mali have been French protectorates in the past. Presently the two African nations have emerged as storm centres of jihadi violence.

Increase in Affiliates of ISIS

An article by Louella Mae Eleftheriou Smith, published in the London-based newspaper, *The Independent,* on December 10, 2015, revealed that the Islamic State has increased its international support base phenomenally in countries ranging from the Philippines to Egypt and beyond. The number of Affiliates of Islamic State across the globe, towards the end of the year 2015, had risen to 42. By now a few more Military Affiliates, or Wilayats, have been added to the old figure.

A map, posted on the website of Times of India World on 10 December, 2015, provides details of the 40 groups which have pledged formal affiliation to the terrorist group ISIS.[11] It further lists 12 more Affiliates that have pledged support to Islamic State, as identified in a Global Terrorism Index report. By now the number of Islamic groups pledging allegiance to ISIS has risen to 63. An up-to-date list of the Affiliates of ISIS is given in the Appendix at the end of this book.

The Global Terrorism Index, created by *The International Institute of Economics and Peace* (IEP), measures the scale and impact of terror attacks across the world. The report, released in November, 2015, revealed that global terrorism has reached its highest level and continues to rise at an "unprecedented pace". The Global Terrorism Index graph, highlighting the growth of Affiliates of ISIS, was also reproduced on the website of *Times of India World* on December 10, 2015.

Lately pro-ISIS factions have also been seen in Algeria and Gaza, while splinter factions from Afghanistan and Pakistan are believed to have sent fighters to the Syria-Iraq battlefields, according to informed sources.

Expanding Footprints in Africa

Another fast rising terrorist group known as Jahba East Africa, pledged allegiance to Islamic State on April 7, 2016.[12] After consolidating its hold in several countries of West Asia, the militant Muslim state is now expanding across Africa. In March 2016, the group Jahba East Africa gave an oath of allegiance, to Al-Baghdadi and recognized him as the rightful Khalifa (Caliph) of all Muslims. The group is believed be made up of former supporters of Al-Shabab, a terrorist group formerly linked to Al Qaeda that controls much of Somalia and has carried out attacks in Kenya and other East African nations. Jahba East Africa urged all Muslim supporters on Twitter on 8 April to join it. A new era will come to East Africa soon, Insha Allah (God willing), the Jahba East Africa group tweeted. It appears that the African continent is likely to emerge as another major storm centre of jihad in the coming years. The region has the potential of exceeding the vast territorial expanse of ISIS in West Asia. The civil society must brace itself to face another turbulent zone of holy war in the coming decades!

Sky News Files Reveal Useful Intelligence

In the second week of March, 2016, thousands of documents detailing the names, phone numbers and family contacts of the ISIS jihadists have surfaced. These crucial files were handed over to the Sky News television channel on 9th March, 2016. Tens of thousands documents were handed over to Sky News by a disillusioned convert to sanity who was formerly working with the group.[13]

The foreign fighters listed in the documents accessed by the Sky News were from at least 51 countries, including some from the United Kingdom. The recruits had to give their personal information when they joined the terror organization. They were required to fill a 23-questions form when they were inducted into the ISIS cadre. A lot of the names and the new names assigned to them by the Islamic State on the registration forms have become known. But the key breakthrough from the documents may come from the information about the identities of a number of previously unknown jihadis ensconced in the UK and the militants embedded across northern

Europe, Middle East and North Africa. Finding their whereabouts and movements is crucial to breaking the jihadi organization and preventing further terror attacks. Many of the men passed through a series of jihadi "hotspots" – such as Yemen, Sudan, Tunisia, Libya, Pakistan and Afghanistan – on multiple occasions, but apparently remained unchecked and unmonitored. They were able to enter Syria to fight and then, return home.[14] One of the files marked "Martyrs" provided details of a brigade manned entirely by the fighters who wanted to carry out suicide attacks and were trained to do so. The man who stole it was a former Free Syrian Army convert to the Islamic State. His name is Abu Hamed.

Pakistani Brigadier Endorses Savagery
The tactical construct of using savagery against kaffirs has been lucidly prescribed in the Islamic scriptures, as highlighted by the retired Pakistani Brigadier S. K. Malik in his book, *The Islamic Concept of War*. On pages 57–60 of his tome he has quoted many Ayats from the Quran advocating the use of savagery to win wars. No wonder, savagery continues to rule the hearts and minds of Al-Baghdadi and his storm-troopers. The gory tradition is faithfully reflected in the public beheadings of innocents and the destruction of churches followed by abductions and rapes of the Christian and Yazidi women. The ISIS Affiliate Boko Haram, which now claims to hold more than 20 thousand square miles territory in Nigeria, is following the same tactics.

Islamic State has emerged as a group of savage soldiers of Islam who behead and maim non-Muslims and Shias. They also murder Muslims who do not believe in Wahhabi tenets, or those who oppose them. They proudly claim that they are doing what is enshrined in the Islamic scriptures and was practiced by the Prophet in his campaigns against the kuffar.

Foreign Fighters Joining ISIS

The well-known analyst Samuel Oakford of Soufan Group revealed in an article that nearly 31,000 volunteers from at least 86 countries have travelled to Syria and Iraq to fight for Islamic State and related extremist groups since 2011.[15] The New York based research consultancy reported that the figure of foreigners joining the Islamic State had roughly doubled since a previous assessment made in the summer of 2014. The latest numbers largely confirmed the earlier estimates made by the US and the United Nations. Approximately half of the foreign fighters hail from the Middle East and North Africa. According to the Soufan Group's latest estimates, some 2,500 fighters were from Saudi Arabia and 4,700 from the former Soviet Union who have been battling in Iraq and Syria since 2011. Militants from Tunisia, numbering nearly 7,000 continue to have an outsized presence in Jihadi groups of Iraq and Syria. In a country of less than 11 million people, such a figure is a huge concern for the officials of Tunisia.

In Europe, 3,700 out of an estimated 5,000 plus fighters reportedly travelled from just four countries: France, Belgium, Germany and the United Kingdom. French officials confirmed that around 1,800 fighters for the Islamic State had proceeded from within their borders, including several who reportedly returned to carry out the November, 2015, terror attacks in Paris that left 130 people dead. The increase in foreign volunteers shows that efforts to contain the flow of foreign recruits to extremists groups in Syria and Iraq had limited impact. In an interview with *VICE News*, Patrick Skinner, Director of Special Projects at the Soufan Group said that the influx of foreigners peaked towards the end of the year 2014.

Patrick Skinner further added that a large portion of those who travelled to Iraq and Syria, between 20 and 30 percent, had retraced their steps, and emerged in their home countries, particularly in

Europe. While that means there could be fewer foreign extremists in both countries than data indicates, it presents a worrying threat, particularly if they were sent back on jihadi missions rather than having given up on fighting for the cause.

Supremacy of Caliph

Historically, and by the time-honored Islamic tradition, the Caliph, or Khalifah, is regarded by every Muslim as the Regent of Allah ordained to rule the world according to the precepts of Islam. The orthopraxy of Islam stipulates that once a Caliphate is established it becomes the Quran-ordained duty of every Muslim across the world to obey the command of the Caliph. The role and authority of the Caliph are elucidated below.

1. The Caliph is authorized by Islamic law and tradition to declare a jihad against 'kaffirs' (all non-Muslims) across the world. Thereafter it becomes the duty of every Muslim to join the holy war to establish the rule of Islam worldwide – as ordained in the Quran.

2. Islam has a unique concept of binding all Muslims of the world together which is called Ummah, i.e., a unique global Islamic fraternity. Ummah forms the bedrock of all pan-Islamic movements, including the holy war called *jihad.* Islam does not recognize national boundaries. For that matter it does not recognize any commitment of affinity to a particular Nation or State. Its affinities are exclusively Islam specific and devoted to religious matters and that makes it an extra-territorial entity, as highlighted by late B. R. Ambedkar in his book, *Pakistan or Partition of India.*

3. A very disquieting aspect of the concept of Ummah is that a Muslim need not have any commitment to fight for his motherland. He has a higher commitment enjoined on him by the Quran, namely his allegiance to the global Muslim entity called Ummah.

As explained by Dr. B. R. Ambedkar in his seminally researched tome, *Pakistan or Partition of India,* in preference to a call to defend his motherland, a Muslim is entitled to seek help of another Muslim nation calling for jihad against the supposed oppression of Muslims. Dr. Ambedkar explained this aspect very lucidly by quoting from the deposition made by the well-known Muslim leader of Khilafat movement, Maulana Mahomed Ali.[16] The Maulana had acquired phenomenal knowledge of the Quran and Islamic law and made a canonical assertion during his trial in the Sessions Court. On July 8, 1921, a strange resolution was passed by the Khilafat Committee at Karachi in which the Maulana had exhorted the Muslims, including the Muslim soldiers of the British Indian army, not to join the battle against the Amir of Afghanistan. For his open defiance of the law he was charged in a Karachi court with preaching sedition against the Indian State. In his address to the Jury in the Sessions Court, Mahomed Ali contested the charges by citing chapter and verse from the Quranic law that Islam does not permit the faithful to fight against the jihadi army of a Muslim ruler like the Amir of Afghanistan. He argued, that in the event of a jihad being declared against 'kaffirs' the law of Islam required that no Muslim should render any assistance against the Islamic warriors (Mujahideen). The learned Maulana further reiterated that if jihadists approached the place or region where Muslims were living, the Muslims must assist the Mujahideen to the best of their ability and power. That was the clear and undisputable law of Islam, averred Maulana Mahomed Ali in his long testimony.

4. In view of the commandments enshrined in the Islamic scriptures, the call of the Caliph Al- Baghdadi seeking total commitment of all Muslims has been attracting thousands of wannabe jihadists from different countries and continents to his mission for global jihad. Al Baghdadi's Quran-based exhortations to the faithful to join his

global jihad have drawn massive response from Muslims across the globe, including several thousand volunteers (including Muslim women) from Europe, USA, Canada and Chechnya – even some foot-soldiers from India. He has already demonstrated his determination to make full use of the strategy to instill terror into the hearts of non-Muslims.

Persecution of Shias

The ISIS has been pursuing a regular war against Shias whom the Sunnis consider heretics who deserve to be killed. Apart from fighting the Shia militant groups, the soldiers of ISIS have been ruthlessly massacring the civilian population of Shias, wherever they find them. Their aim appears to be to consolidate the Sunni militant groups under their wings for pitting them against the Shias. After capturing Mosul in June, 2014, the Islamic State's army advanced towards Baghdad. Several videos were released by the Islamic State's media department boasting of massacres of Shias and Christians. While some human rights activists placed the number of the Shias massacred in Tikrit during the three days long battle at around 560-770, the Islamic State claimed that they had massacred nearly 1,700 Shia soldiers in Tikrit alone. Almost all of them were fresh recruits who had joined the Iraqi Army, but had not completed their training.

Ideology of ISIS

The Islamic State rigorously follows the Salafist doctrine of jihad. For them there is no distinction between the Islamic religion and the state. All decisions of ISIS are based on the hardline interpretation of the Quran and Islamic scriptures. The decisions taken are then rigorously enforced in the areas controlled by the Islamic State. Broadly the ideology of the ISIS is the same as of the Al-Qaeda, the Taliban and Wahhabis of Saudi Arabia.

It may be recalled that Salafism as a movement began in Egypt. Its ideological forefathers were the same as those of the Muslim Brotherhood. It continued to grow side by side with Wahhabism - the doctrine of Mohammed Ibn Abd al-Wahhab of Arabia who died in 1792. He was the Islamic preacher whose interpretation of the Quran became the state doctrine of Saudi Arabia. Salafism and Wahhabism are very closely connected because of the influence of Muslim Brotherhood-linked clerics straddling Saudi Arabia. Salafist ideology draws extensively from the writings and thoughts of Ibn Taymiyya, the well-known fourteenth century Islamic jurist. Although Sayyid Qutb, who was the renowned ideologue of Muslim Brotherhood had been hanged in 1966 by President Nasser of Egypt, his ideas and strategy have left an abiding imprint on several jihadi groups, including the newly formed Islamic State. Syed Qutb used to consider all those who did not strictly adhere to the Sharia law as belonging to the pre-Islamic period of 'jahilliya' or darkness. He, therefore, advocated the overthrowing of all such regimes and replacing them with Sharia-compliant Islamic states.

Goals of ISIS

The Islamic State has rapidly morphed into a reasonably well organized country, commanding sovereignty over a sizeable territory. It has acquired an independent entity. The Caliph Al-Baghdadi has drawn up a charter of goals: short term, medium term and long term. He proposes to march to these milestones by management of savagery and recourse to vexation and exhaustion of kaffirs. Thus the Islamic State is determined to carry forward Islam's war without borders. Its short term goal is to consolidate itself in the areas it has already seized and to capture more territory in Syria, Iraq, Libya and Nigeria, including in the far away Caucasus. Indonesia, and the Philippines.

The medium term goal of ISIS is to advance into the neighbouring Sunni States. Perhaps countries like Jordan, Yemen and Saudi Arabia which are supported by western powers may be its next targets. It could target even Pakistan to bring it under Wilayat Khorasan to threaten India. These Islamic countries are controlled by authoritarian dictators whose rule is resented by radicalised Muslim young men.

The third and the ultimate goal of the ISIS is well-defined and widely publicized. It is enshrined in the Islamic scriptures and aims at conquering and dominating the entire world by converting the globe into Dar-ul-Islam. The ISIS wants to take over and rule over what they perceive as the Islamic universe.

Doctrine Called Baqiyya-Wa-Tatamaddad

As highlighted by the European Council of Foreign Relations, the ambitious slogan of the Islamic State is 'baqiyya-*wa tatamaddad*' which signifies its objective of "remaining steady and continue expanding". The slogan is indicative of the group's aggressive and expansionist goal. Its origin lies in the hoary history of Islam's kinetic strategy of holding on to the countries conquered and then moving forward for greater conquests. The self-proclaimed Caliph, who demands total allegiance of all Muslims, wants first to encompass and consolidate the entire Muslim world and eventually to subsume the whole world under his domination. This global goal has been circulated among members and supporters since the group's birth, when it styled itself the Islamic State of Iraq.[17] The strategy called *baqiyya wa tatamaddad* was followed throughout the history of Islam. In those days, the ambitions of the jihadis were etched clearly on the black flag of the Prophet, with graphics of the globe under the group's banner.

It is well-known that Lebanon, Jordan, Palestine and Israel, along with Syria and Iraq continue to be in the sights of al-Baghdadi. It is crystal clear that the ISIS will seek continuous expansion by waging holy war for several years. Of greatest concern to India, however, is its strategy of conquering Afghanistan and then over-running Pakistan. The establishment of Wilayat Khorasan is a step forward towards subjugating India by destroying the Hindu faith, as ordained in the Islamic scriptures. The ISIS is determined to capitalize on the fact that the three targeted countries, Afghanistan, Pakistan and India, have multiple radical Islamic outfits which will willingly opt for jihad against Hindus when the black banners of Islam come calling from Khorasan via Pakistan.

The expanding reach of the Islamic State was reflected in the seven bomb attacks which rattled the Indonesian capital Jakarta, on 14th January, 2016, and claimed seven lives, including that of a police officer. The gun battle between the attackers and the security forces lasted more than three hours. The attack demonstrated how the ISIS has progressed deep into Indonesia. There are rumors that it is now trying to expand its area of operations in Malaysia and Thailand.

The global plans of the Islamic State are focused on annexing the entire Middle East, seizing Europe and thereafter overrunning India, say during the next five years. The group also wants to control the Muslim-dominated parts of the African continent. After conquering West Asia, the continents of Africa and Europe are their major targets.

Administrative Structure of Islamic State

After declaration of the Caliphate on the first Friday of Ramadan in 2014, Al-Baghdadi gave a speech in the historic Al-Nouri mosque of Mosul exhorting all Muslims to obey him. For effectively administering the Caliphate, he appointed a number of advisors and military commanders. Each one of them has been assigned a well-defined responsibility. There are two Deputy Commanders working under Al-Baghdadi. One of them looks after the conquered areas of Syria, while the other is in charge of the territory seized in Iraq. They are advised by sort of a cabinet, or Majlis-e-Shoora, comprising a number of salaried Ministers. Each one of them has been assigned a specific responsibility, e.g., to look after the Departments of Transport, Internal Security, Treasury, etc. In addition there is a separate Minister to administer the foreign jihadi fighters and cater to their needs. Due to security concerns Caliph Al-Baghdadi rarely appears in public.

Al-Baghdadi has organized a War Office to manage the jihadi campaign, including administration of logistics. Many of his Ministers and Troop Commanders are known to have served during the regime of Saddam Hussein as high-ranking officers. Many others have high level military expertise which is reflected at all levels of the Islamic State's war machine. There are approximately one thousand medium to top level field commanders each one of whom is reportedly paid a salary ranging from $300 to $3000 per month depending on the duties assigned to them.

A Governor administers every province and is accountable to the Caliph. The ISIS has been rapidly building the requisite infrastructure to provide all essential services to the people like healthcare, education and the maintenance of public order. It also has a number of courts based on the Sharia law. The Syrian city of Raqqa has been functioning as the *de facto* capital of the Islamic State.

Financial Stability of Islamic State

Providing municipal services, health care and transport facilities cost big money. But that is no constraint for the Islamic State which has now become the richest terrorist organization in the world. Its income (estimated to be at least $1 to $2 million per day) is primarily derived from the sale and smuggling of oil, supplemented by extortions, kidnappings, and poll tax imposed on dhimmis (non-Muslims) living in the area it controls. The outfit is largely self-financing, with donations making up a tiny percentage of its total income. According to the Center for the Analysis of Terrorism, the Islamic State made nearly $2.4 billion in the year 2015. Despite losing some territory in recent times, the ISIS continues to be the richest terrorist group on the planet. It still has an over $2 billion financial empire. The authors of the report claim that the military defeat of the ISIS is not imminent because its economic collapse is nowhere in sight.[18]

ISIS Evolves into a Viable State

A leaked internal Islamic State manual show the manner in which ISIS has managed to set up a state in Iraq and Syria complete with government departments, a treasury and an economic programme for self-sufficiency. The document has a blueprint for establishing foreign relations, a full-fledged propaganda mechanism and centralized control over oil, gas and the other vital parts of the economy. Behind the death cult image of the Islamic State the details of organizing a bureaucracy have been worked out by Al Baghdadi's team.

The manual captioned, *'Principles in the Administration of the Islamic State'*, recounts the state-restructuring aspirations of ISIS and the ways in which it has managed to set itself apart as the richest and the most dangerous jihadi group of the past 50 years. The document reads like a master plan for consolidating power in a Sharia-compliant State. Although sworn to the founding Islamic principle of brutal violence, the ISIS is equally concerned about mundane matters such as health, education, commerce, communications and jobs. It was written as a foundational text to train cadres of administrators soon after the ISIS leader, Al-Baghdadi, declared a Caliphate on 28th June, 2014. It spells out how to organize government departments including education, natural resources, industry, foreign affairs, public relations and military camps. It further details how ISIS will build separate training camps for regular troops and veteran fighters. Veterans, it says, should go on a fortnight's refresher course each year to receive instruction in the latest arts of using weapons, military planning and military technologies.

The document reveals for the first time that the ISIS always wanted to train children in the arts of war. Propaganda videos have been showing children being drilled, and even being made to shoot the captive kaffirs. The children are receiving training on bearing light arms and outstanding performers will be selected for security portfolio assignments, including the manning of the checkpoints and for being deployed as patrols.[19]

The Islamic State combines the resolve of Osama bin Laden laced with the brutal strategies used in the medieval era. And ISIS promises to deliver to its fighters what the Muslim conquerors have been offering to the believers for the past 1,400 years, i.e., loot and captive kaffir women. The promise of heaven after death and the allurement of amassing riches, including capturing women through victory on earth is a heady brew. The same age-old temptation is being used today, to entice and recruit perverse young men!

Coins Minted Hoping to Conquer Rome and USA

ISIS has started minting its own gold and silver coins, as depicted in an hour-long video titled, *"The Rise of the Khilafah and the Return of the Gold Dinar,"* released by them. It claims that these coins will replace the 'satanic' concept of banks. The video is in English with Arabic subtitles and begins with an analysis of "the capitalist financial system of enslavement, underpinned by a piece of paper called the Federal Reserve dollar note." and the corruption that allowed for the American destruction of the monetary system intended by Allah.

The new ISIS currency will come in several denominations of silver, gold and copper. The coins are being imprinted with Islamic symbols and will be completely devoid of human and animal images in accordance with Sharia law. The reverse side of a coin shows seven wheat stalks, representing the blessing of spending in the path of

Allah. Another coin has been imprinted with a map of the world, representing the total territory which Caliph's soldiers would capture, including Constantinople, Rome and America. Another coin has a spear and shield depicting that the source of the black flags of Prophet Mohammad was for jihad in the name of Allah."[20]

Russia Joins War against ISIS

The war against the Islamic State took a new turn on September 30, 2015, when Russia decided to attack the ISIS with its latest aircraft. Within first two days, Russian planes destroyed a number of installations and killed nearly 300 jihadists. Fighter planes were sent to Bashar Al-Assad's strongholds in Syria. The Russian President, Putin, is believed to have discussed the issue with Barack Obama. The Russian Parliament formally approved the military intervention against the Islamic State and approved deployment of its advanced fighter planes to Syria. The air strikes were followed by a call from Vladimir Putin for mobilizing 1,50,000 conscripts into the Russian army - perhaps for rushing to Syria and joining the battle on ground, if necessary. The Russian government also announced the creation of an "Information Center" in Baghdad to co-ordinate its anti-ISIS operations with officers from Syria and Iraq.[21]

Russian intelligence sources feel that the situation is likely to worsen in Turkmenistan, Tajikistan, Uzbekistan, Afghanistan and Xinjiang-Uyghur Region of China. It was reported by the UK based newspaper, *Daily Express,* that Russia's Spy Chief, Alexander Bortnikov, warned that fighters from the Taliban, many of whom have pledged allegiance to ISIS, were heavily armed and prepared to pass through porous border controls. Many Russian analysts are apprehensive that the jihadi groups might try to open up a new front to the north of its territories after being pegged back in Syria by Russian airstrikes. The invasion would be a swipe at Vladimir Putin as it would take ISIS into the former Soviet states of Turkmenistan,

Uzbekistan and Tajikistan, which are beholden to Moscow for protective security cover. Historically, Central Asia has been a region of long standing geopolitical conflicts.

In October, 2015, Putin had described the situation in Afghanistan as "close to critical" and called on other ex-Soviet nations to be prepared to act together to repel a possible attack by Islamic State. But the anticipated attack on Central Asian Republics, which constitute soft underbelly of Russia, did not happen.

ISIS Gains in Afghanistan

In recent times the ISIS has made substantial territorial gains in several provinces of Afghanistan, including the notorious Tora Bora region. The development has forced the United States to significantly intensify its bombing campaign in Afghanistan during the past two months. According to senior military commanders, Islamic State militants, after seizing many territories outside of Iraq and Syria, are now making inroads into Afghanstan.[22] According to the data compiled by the US Air Force, drones and fighter jets dropped 251 bombs and missiles in January and February, 2016, in Afghanistan. That was more than three times the air strikes in the same period last year. The Bureau of Investigative Journalism, a private organization that tracks airstrikes, said that between 332 and 359 people have been killed in American air attacks in January and February, 2016, which is five times the number killed in the first two months of 2015.

Many Islamic State militants in Afghanistan happen to be former members of the Pakistani Taliban. The real danger to peace in Afghanistan comes from the Taliban soldiers shifting their loyalty to Islamic State. The Afghan and American commanders admit that today the Taliban appear to be stronger than at any other point since 2001. They have nearly 20,000 to 40,000 fighters. Their estimated strength is said to be much higher than the number of militants aligned with Islamic State. But ISIS is feverishly trying to catch up with the Taliban numbers. A message indicating the future intentions of ISIS in Afghanistan and Pakistan was delivered loud and clear, through three attacks – one in Afghanistan and two in Pakistan. On 27th March, 2016, there was an attack on the Christians celebrating Easter in Lahore by Jamaat-ul Ahrar, a group aligned with Islamic State. The second attack by ISIS took place in the third week of July, 2016, on members of the Hazara community demonstrating in Kabul resulting in the killing 80 Shias. There was a third attack on 8 August, 2016, targeting Pakistani lawyers in a hospital in Quetta which killed 74 persons. The ISIS took the responsibility for the killings.

The escalation of jihadi activities in Afghanistan has given rise to serious dangers to Russia as well as India. There are numerous criminal groups included in the Taliban Movement on the northern borders of the country. Some of them have also began operating under the black flag of the Islamic State which has led to a sharp rise in the threat of terrorists invading Central Asia – the soft underbelly of Russia.

Recently ISIS militants in eastern Afghanistan have taken to the airwaves to win recruits in an attempt to gather strength and replace the Taliban as the leading force in the Islamic insurgency.[23] This development has been creating concern in official circles because it may encourage young people to join the radical movement.

The 90-minute daily broadcast, called, *"Voice of the Caliphate"*, in Pushto language consists mainly of interviews and messages eulogizing the ISIS. It can be heard in Nangarhar, the eastern province where ISIS has established its stronghold. It controls several districts wrested from the Taliban, who are seeking to re-establish their regime after being toppled by US-led military intervention in 2001. A spokesman of the group, Jan Aqa Shafaq, contemptuously remarked that most of the Muslim youth had become 'lipstick young men' who shave closely and wear the kind of clothing that does not distinguish them from females.

ISIS is a relatively new force in strife-torn Afghanistan and there are contradictory assessments about its actual strength. No one knows how strong it is and how closely its operations are linked with the main arm in Iraq and Syria. Security officials say that many members of the ISIS in Afghanistan happen to be former Taliban fighters who fell out with the current leadership. Some were those who are seeking a more extreme form of militant activity. The lone-wolf attack mounted by the ISIS on Pakistan's Consulate in Jalalabad in the Nangarhar Province in the second week of January, 2016, showed the rapid growth of the allurement for joining the ranks of ISIS in the sensitive region.

In the third week of December, 2015, the Commander of the International forces in Afghanistan, US General John Campbell, said there were between 1,000 to 3,000 members of the ISIS under cover in Afghanistan. He warned that its influence would spread if it was left unchecked.

Officials in Nangarhar confessed that they were unable to block the broadcasts because the operators tend to shift the location of the source of mischief. They relocate from one place to another, averred Attaullah Khogyani, a spokesman for the Governor of Nangarhar province. Meanwhile, Ahmed Ali Hazrat, Head of the Provincial Council in Nangarhar said that as most of the Afghan youth have remained jobless, the radio broadcasts would attract them to join the ISIS. He warned that the troops of Daesh (Islamic State) were only seven kilometers away from Jalalabad and if the government did not act soon the outfit would expand its broadcast range and recruit young men even from Kabul.[24]

A Pentagon report and the recent assessment of Gen. John Campbell (top Commander of U.S. Forces in the country) confirmed that the ISIS branch in Afghanistan, known as the Khorasan Province IS-KP), has become very active in Nangarhar, which lies just along the Pakistan border. Khorasan is the ancient name of the region which in medieval times covered large areas of Afghanistan, Pakistan, Iran, and parts of northern India. A top Russian military official has estimated that nearly 3,000 ISIS-linked militants are operating in Afghanistan.

Radio Free Europe Radio Liberty (RFERL) reported that ISIS' Khorasan Province recently conquered a new territory in Nangarhar, prompting many residents to flee their homes. The Khorasan Wilayat has seized pockets of terrain from the Taliban in Nangarhar Province and is growing by recruiting "disaffected Taliban" and others, noted the Pentagon report. Some volunteers of the ethnic Uzbek minority in Afghanistan are also believed to be fighting alongside ISIS.

In September, 2015, the United Nations reported that ISIS has been actively recruiting followers in nearly three-quarters of the 34 provinces which means that 25 provinces of Afghanistan now have an ISIS presence.

In the third week of December, 2015, the Commander of the International forces in Afghanistan, US General John Campbell, said there were between 1,000 to 3,000 members of the ISIS nestling in Afghanistan. He warned that the group's influence would spread if it was left unchecked. In recent times the ISIS has made substantial territorial gains in several provinces of Afghanistan, including the notorious Tora Bora region. This development forced the United States to significantly intensify its bombing campaign in Afghanistan for two months. The assessment of General Campbell was proved to be correct. On 23 July, 2016, two suicide bombers attacked a procession of Hazara Muslims in Kabul. The processionists were agitating for the laying of electricity lines through the Herat region which is their stronghold. In the attack, 80 Hazaras were killed and nearly 200 injured. Hazaras are Shia Muslims and therefore deemed to be apostates by Salafi Muslims. The Islamic State promptly claimed that they were behind the attack, which demonstrated the growing clout of the ISIS in Afghanistan. This was one of the worst ISIS bombings in Afghanistan.

CHAPTER 2

Human Right Abuses by the ISIS

"Islam never was for a day the religion of peace ….. [but] of war. Your Prophet …was ordered with war till Allah is worshipped alone."

– Al-Baghdadi, cited by Andrew Hosken in his book 'Empire of Fear'

The ultra-radical group ISIS has left a trail of indescribable brutalities in its march through the Middle East, Nigeria, Tunisia and Libya. Its soldiers have been killing and maiming thousands of innocents and circulating videos of beheadings, ritualized rapes, torture and murder carried out by warriors of Islam. The victims are those who do not subscribe to what they call true Islam, i.e., the faith as preached and practiced by Prophet Muhammad.

One of their worst acts of brutal savagery was the public beheading of an 83 year old archaeologist, Khalid al-Asaad, in August, 2015. Khalid Assad was a globally respected keeper of the ancient ruins in the Syrian city of Palmyra. He was killed for his so-called anti-Islamic crimes like attending some "infidel conferences" and serving as "director of idolatry".[1] It is difficult to ignore the systematic destruction of several historical sites by ISIS, especially the demolition of one of the grandest relics in the ancient ruins of Palmyra - the Temple of Baalshamin.

Anne Bernard, a correspondent of *Time* magazine pointed out that the destruction of antiquities in Syria and Iraq has reached staggering proportions, causing an irreversible loss to the world heritage. For ISIS, the destruction of the Palmyra temple, like the destruction of ancient statues and monuments in Nimrud, Hatra and other regions, is a part of lawful erosion of the symbols of "apostates". It is part of an ethnic, religious and cultural cleansing of anything which the zealots deem alien to the pure Islam.

According to Donatella Rovera, the Senior Crisis Response Adviser of Amnesty International, the Islamic State has been carrying out innumerable despicable crimes. Its soldiers have transformed rural areas of the Sinjar Mountain (the home of Yazidis) into blood-soaked killing fields by their brutal campaign to obliterate all traces of non-Arab faiths and non-Sunni Muslims.[2]

Soon after seizing large tracts of Syria, the soldiers of ISIS started targeting the minority groups. All Christians, descendants of the indigenous pre-Christ Assyrian population, who have lived in Iraq for at least 3,000 years, were driven out from Mosul. Their homes were marked with the Arabic letter *nun*, an abbreviation for the Nazarene (or Nasrani), a term which refers to Christians.

After over-running Mosul, the ISIS vehicles driving through the streets of Mosul announced on loudspeakers that there were three choices available for Christians: pay jizya, i.e., a special tax for Christians fixed at $470 per person (an amount that most could not afford to pay), or convert to Islam, or die. The announcement made the entire Christian community flee the region.

In August 2014, thousands of Yazidis, an ancient minority indigenous to northern Iraq, were ruthlessly slaughtered by the fighters of the Islamic state because they were deemed idol-worshipping 'satans'. Tens of thousands of them, driven out from their homes, were trapped on Mount Sinjar with no food or water. All sides of the mountain were sealed by the jihadists leaving no escape route. Eventually Kurdish forces backed by the US airstrikes were able to rescue most of those trapped, but not before hundreds fell to exposure, thirst and the bullets of ISIS.

Donatella Rovera of the Amnesty International who has visited northern Iraq, said, that the massacres and abductions being carried out by the Islamic State provided harrowing evidence that a new wave of ethnic cleansing against minorities was sweeping across northern Iraq.[3]

Gender Segregation and Female Persecution

In true Islamic style, gender segregation is rigorously enforced in the Islamic State. Every woman is compelled to wear the veil while appearing in public. The morality police, known as the Hisbah, patrol the streets to ensure that Sharia law is being followed. Alcohol, tobacco and drugs are banned. Punishments for various transgressions of Sharia law include flogging, amputation of limbs and death. By displaying raw violence in public squares, a high level of fear is created among citizens. This display of raw savagery is included in their propaganda campaign, too. The Islamic State has been circulating gruesome videos of mass killings, individual assassinations, including the beheadings of American journalists James Foley and Stephen Sotloff and an aid worker from the United Kingdom. The on-camera beheadings are used for publicizing their ruthlessness as a strategy to motivate the religious-minded young Muslims.

ISIS Jihadi Executes Own Mother

An extremely brutal instance of raw savagery came from the town of Raqqa in January, 2016. According to newspaper reports an ISIS jihadi, Ali Saqr al-Qasem, executed his own mother in public after she tried to persuade him to quit the group. The Syrian Observatory for

Human Rights, which monitors the war in Syria from London, said that a number of reliable local sources informed them of the killing.[4] The activist group, 'Raqqa *is Being Slaughtered Silently (RBSS)* ', also reported the incident. It said that Ali Saqr al-Qasem, 20, shot his mother, Leena, in the head with an assault rifle in front of a large crowd. Leena's fault was that she wanted to leave Raqqa and had asked her son to come out with her. The son reported her to the group. She was ordered to be executed on the ground of 'inciting her son to betray the ISIS' by leaving Raqqa. She was executed near the main post office building where she used to work. Hundreds of people gathered to witness the killing, as is common with such events in the Islamic State.

The ISIS is believed to have executed a number of women, including Ruqia Hassan, a "citizen journalist" from Raqqa who reported on life inside the town, on her Facebook page. Those who become subjects of the nascent Islamic state have to obey Sharia law or face fierce penalties. Beatings and lashes are common. In Mosul, the group shot a female doctor for refusing to wear a headscarf. Subsequently they shot two more female doctors for refusing to treat Islamic State fighters.[5.]

The official mouthpiece of ISIS in English, Dabiq, is an e-magazine which has been named after a village in Syria. According to a belief among jihadists after the formation of Wilayat Khorasan, the final battle for supremacy of Islam will be won in Dabiq village. The slick and e-magazine *Dabiq* is being used for publicizing stories of the success of the Islamic State. The name of the magazine has been taken from a location described in the Islamic legend. The objective is to capitalize on the folklore to enhance the Islamic State's appeal for seeking more recruits.

Rape is routinely practiced in the style of medieval Islam for humiliating and subjugating the womenfolk of conquered populations. It is also used to 'reward' the fighters for services rendered to the caliphate. Women as young as fourteen years are given as 'gifts' to ISIS commanders, while others are sold as slaves in the marketplace. It is not known how many women have been captured by the Islamic State. The number, however, is believed to be in the thousands. They are being beaten, tortured, raped, sold and re-sold.

According to Haleh Esfandiari, Director of the Middle East Program at the Woodrow Wilson International Center for Scholars, ISIS soldiers take the older women to makeshift slave markets to sell. The younger girls are raped or married off to fighters. This practice is based on the Islamic concept of temporary marriages. Once the ISIS fighters have had sex with these young girls, they just pass them on to other soldiers. Sometime the girls who have been captured are forced to call their parents and recount over the phone what is being done to them as a form of enhanced torture. Many girls are held in a secret prison in Mosul which was used to massacre the Shias when fighters of the Islamic State first arrived. Those who convert to Islam are sold to jihadist fighters as 'brides', sometime for as little as $25. Captured girls who refuse to convert are raped, beaten and eventually killed.

Atrocities on Yazidis

The worst victims of the savagery of the ISIS have been Yazidis who are a helpless minority in Iraq, Kurdistan and neighboring countries. The Yazidis are a Kurdish speaking people who live principally in northern Iraq. Reviled as devil worshipers for centuries by their Muslim and Christian neighbors, they have endured over 70 genocides in which over 20 million Yazidis are estimated to have perished. Most Yazidis have been compelled to abandon their faith and culture. They are traditional worshippers of the Peacock Angel or Taus Malik and claim to have originated in India and Iran. It is said that Malik Taus, or Peacock Angel, is the Yazidi symbol of the Hindu God Murugan, or Karthikeyan, the elder son of Shiva and Adishakti. The Muslims of

West Asia and soldiers of the Islamic State consider them devil-worshippers, fit to be killed for their pagan religious beliefs. Many Indologists, including the America-based well-known researcher, Dr. Subhash Kak, feel that the Yazidis have an Indian past.

Immediately after formation of the Caliphate in 2014 the ISIS launched a campaign to destroy the cities and villages inhabited by Yazidis. It has allegedly murdered nearly 3,000 of them and sold 4,500 women and girls belonging to the bedraggled community into sex-slavery. Many of the abducted girls committed suicide. Yazidis have no country which will own them. Most of them were trapped by the ISIS around their traditional habitat at Mount Sinjar. Thousands of Yazidis were hunted, killed and taken prisoners. As a rule, all captured Yazidi men are simply shot dead, unless they convert to Islam and join the ISIS troops.

Travails of a Yazidi Girl

An eighteen years old Yazidi girl, Jinan, who survived a brutal ordeal at the hands of the militant jihadists of the Islamic State is the co-writer of a book in French titled "Esclave de Daesh" ("Daesh's Slave"). She authored the book with the help of a French journalist, Thierry Oberle and has explained to the AFP (*Agence France-Presse*) how she was kidnapped, beaten, sold, and raped. According to her, ISIS militants run an international market in Iraq where Yazidi and Christian women are sold as if they were cattle. Jinan was captured in early 2014 and held by militants of the Islamic State for three months before she managed to flee after stealing a key of the room in which she was imprisoned. She has explained in the book how, after being captured, she was moved around to a number of locations before being bought by two men, a former police officer and an Imam. She described to the *Agence France-Presse* (AFP) how she and some other Yazidi prisoners were locked up in a house. The ISIS soldiers tortured them and tried to forcefully convert them.[6] The hapless girls were chained outdoors in the sun and forced to drink water with dead mice in it. In her book, Jinan describes how once, in Mosul, she was led into a massive reception hall with large columns where dozens of women were gathered. The fighters moved among the girls, laughing raucously and pinching their backsides. She said that one man had commented, saying that one of the girls had big breasts and looked good, but he wanted a Yazidi girl with blue eyes and pale skin. He had added that he was willing to pay the requisite price.

During such "slave markets" Jinan saw not only Iraqis and Syrians but also some westerners whose nationality she could not discern. The best-looking girls were reserved for the bosses of militants or wealthy clients from Gulf nations.

Once she had been sold, Jinan's days were punctuated by men's visits to the house where she was imprisoned along with other women.

Fighters came to make purchases in the foyer where traders acted as intermediaries between the slave owners and Emirs who inspected the girls as if they were inspecting "livestock," Jinan wrote in the book. "I will exchange your Beretta pistol for the brunette," one of the traders had said. "If you prefer to pay cash it is $150 (133 euros). You can also pay in Iraqi dinars."

Convinced that the Yazidi girl did not know Arabic, the two owners of Jinan spoke freely in front of her, and one night she heard a conversation revealing the extent to which the slave trade was being run like an organized business. The conversation between the two men was like this: "A man cannot purchase more than three women, unless he is from Syria, Turkey, or a Gulf nation," said one militant, named Abou Omar. "It's good for business," replied the other man named Abou Anas. "A Saudi buyer has transport and big food costs which a member of the Islamic State does not have. He has a higher quota to make his purchases profitable." The two jihadists had concluded that it was a good deal: The Islamic State increases its profits to support the mujahideen and foreign buyers are satisfied.

After managing to escape, Jinan made her way back to her husband and is now living in a Yazidi refugee camp in Iraqi Kurdistan.

According to *Fox News*, in the first week of June, 2016, nineteen Yazidi girls were burnt alive by the ISIS because they refused to have sex with the jihadis.[7] They were held captive in iron cages and burnt alive while hundreds of people watched helplessly. "They were punished for refusing to have sex with ISIS militants," local activist Abdullah al-Malla told ARA *News*, a Syrian news agency.

Chilling Massacre of Nuns in Yemen

A chilling account of the massacre of the Nuns of the Missionaries of Charity by ISIS came from Yemen on March 4, 2016. The head of the Mission, Sister Sally, who survived the ISIS attack on an old-age home in Yemen has provided a brief account of the gruesome killings in her note.[8]

Sister Sally of the Missionaries of Charity, an order that was founded by Mother Teresa of Calcutta (now Kolkata), miraculously survived the horrendous dance of death unleashed by the ISIS attackers. The report given by the Sister to her superiors, details how Islamic-State gunmen "tied them up, shot them in the head and smashed their heads." She revealed how, after realizing it would be impossible to run to the Convent to warn of the attack, she hid in the refrigerator room. Her hand-written report began by saying that when "ISIS dressed in blue, killed a guard and driver, five young Ethiopian men (Christians) began running to warn the sisters that the ISIS had come to kill them. They were killed one by one. The ISIS intruders tied them to trees, shot them in the head and smashed their heads...."

Sister Sally saw many sisters and helpers killed. The ISIS men were already getting into the convent so she went into the refrigerator room since the door was open. The ISIS men kept searching for her everywhere, as they knew there were five nuns in the old-age home. Sixteen people were killed in the attack, including four of the five nuns. The report notes the order of the nuns was the only Christian presence in Aden. And the ISIS wanted to get rid of all Christians. That statement was corroborated by the fact that the jihadists "smashed and destroyed" all Christian artifacts at the site including the altar, the crucifix, statues, and the Bibles.[9]

Such brutalities are not unique to the ISIS. Savagery has been a part of the history of Islam, as lucidly explained by Yasmin Khatib, an outspoken Egyptian scholar. For instance, the incessant attacks on India by Muslim invaders beginning with the invasion of Sind by Muhammad bin Qasim, followed by Mahmud Ghazanvi and Muhammad Ghori, involved limitless savagery. The plunder and pillage unleashed in 1398 by Timurlane and his troops across Delhi had resulted in the destruction of countless temples and the slaughter of nearly one lakh Hindus. It was another instance of maddening savagery. That ghastly carnage was no different from what ISIS is doing in the 21st Century. In the last century the Nazis too, wreaked enormous havoc on the Jews and several other nations that stood in the way of their expansionist goals.

Beheadings in The Philippines

The Moro Islamic Liberation Front of Philippines captured three non-Muslim tourists in September, 2015. They were held as hostages for seven months by the Abu Sayyaf faction.[10] Among them were two Canadians, a Norwegian and a Filipina. An announcement was made that they would be beheaded on Monday the 25th April, 2016, by an Islamic State affiliated outfit called the Abu Sayyaf group and the video posted on Internet. The faction, which pledged allegiance first to Al-Qaeda and then switched loyalty to Islamic State, set a deadline for receiving a ransom of £4.5 million to be paid for the three captives.[11] Soon videos began emerging in which three haggard-looking men were shown pleading with their families and governments to pay ransom money to the ISIS. One jihadi was shown pressing a machete to their necks, while other armed men stood behind them carrying assault weapons and the distinctive black flag of the Islamic State. True to their penchant for savagery, the Moro Islamic Liberation Front beheaded John Ridsdel, the captive Canadian hostage, on 25th March, 2016, after the Canadian government refused to pay the ransom. Subsequently, they allegedly killed the other captive Canadian.

Chapter 3

Long Reach of Islamic State

Though the announcement by the ISIS about the formation of a Caliphate under Abu Bakr Al-Baghdadi in June 2014 had caused enormous consternation among strategic analysts across the world, the full implications of the impending Islamic savagery were not understood. Most political column-writers and strategic analysts considered the development as the birth of another new Muslim group or country for waging jihad against kaffirs. Apart from the creation of yet another radical Muslim entity, the Caliphate, presided over by Al-Baghdadi, has certain far reaching and ominous implications for many non-Muslim nations, including India. Some of these are analyzed and discussed in the following paragraphs.

Massive Use of Social Media

Social media is being extensively used by almost all jihadi groups to influence the Muslim youth of India, Pakistan, Bangladesh and West Asia. During the last two years ISIS has emerged as the most prolific user of social media for motivating Muslim youth to join them to wage a global jihad against all non-Muslim nations across the globe. On March 6, 2015, a strategic analyst, John Hall, posted an article on the website of *Mail Online* highlighting that web-savvy militants, fighting for the Islamic State in Syria and Iraq, controlled as many as 90,000 Twitter accounts worldwide.[1] These accounts were being used to propagate the success story of the ISIS. They were able to exert an outsized impact on how the world perceives them because of their shrewd use of social media and a large number of online followers.

The widespread reach of Internet, its anonymity, and the difficulties encountered in tracing the source have made social media an ideal tool in the hands of terror groups like the ISIS. In fact, the internet no longer remains just a tool. Often it is also the target of cyber-attacks for stealing useful information. Governments across the world are increasingly facing threats from the cyber world because terrorist outfits now use hacking and sophisticated computer viruses to attack the cyber infrastructure of the targeted nation.

A study of the Twitter accounts undertaken between September and December, 2014, by researchers of the Washington-based Brookings Institute concluded that there were between 46,000 and 70,000 Twitter accounts of the users of Internet supporting the ISIS. The researchers estimated that the true figure of ISIS-related Twitter accounts could be near about 90,000. The Brookings' analysis was based on robust data collected from about 50,000 accounts, and partial information gathered from another 1.9 million accounts. The ISIS militants have been using the social media for impacting the global news and also to assess how the world perceives them. They circulate alluring propaganda online and use social networks to recruit volunteers. As soon as one account is deleted, ISIS supporters manage to set up another.

According to the Brookings report, the locations of only a small number of accounts could be identified because most of the account holders had switched off their operations. But among those that could be located, the vast majority were in the Middle East and North Africa. Some were found in the UK, France, Spain, Italy, Switzerland, Belgium and Australia, too. But these numbers were in single figures, the report found. The two academics, J.M. Berger and technologist Jonathon Morgan of the Brookings Institute claimed that while no mainstream social media platform wanted its services to be used to further the acts of horrific violence, they suspected that some social media sites were not bothered about the challenge of evolving a coherent counter to the problem. The Brookings report emphasized the need for governments and social media companies joining hands to find new ways to tackle the problem of pro-ISIS accounts spreading the display of horrific murder videos and threatening images. The study noted that some social media platforms, including Facebook and YouTube, had already introduced certain measures for preventing the circulation of extremist material. Twitter also had started suspending accounts linked to ISIS by the time the research was started. Although the debates of this issue often tend to fault government intervention as an infringement of free speech, in reality most social media companies currently regulate speech on their platforms.

Tech Magazine & Cryptography

A group of German-speaking jihadists has released the first issue of an online magazine that provides information on encrypted communications and Internet security. The name of the magazine is Kybernetiq. The magazine's release highlights the growing awareness about the importance of security and encryption among Islamist militants. They are keen to use it as a tool to help them operate and spread propaganda undetected. The apparent effort of jihadists is to evade monitoring by government security services.

The magazine, Kybernetiq, is in German. It was released on social media on December 28, 2015, by a group that claims on its Twitter account to be "not ISIS," an acronym referring to the Islamic State group. The group told Radio Free Europe Radio Liberty in a direct message exchange on Twitter that "it is enough for you to know that we aren't from ISIS" but would not say if they had an affiliation with any other militant group.

According to the SITE Intelligence group, which translated extracts from the magazine, Kybernetiq, it includes an article on how jihadists can protect their identities online. One piece of advice tells the would-be militants to avoid applications that have "a mujahid branding," - i.e., a distinct jihadi identity that would identify them as militants by the law enforcement agencies.

The cyber magazine Kybernetiq also recommended that jihadists should use *Tor or Tails*, a free software that enables users to surf the Internet anonymously. The cyber magazine Kybernetiq advised would-be militants to use the WhatsApp or Telegram messaging apps, which have built-in encryption, and praised the GNU Privacy Guard cryptographic software as a "nightmare for intelligence agencies," according to a translation by SITE.

Security-Expert Jihadis

Encrypted platforms like Tor and popular messaging apps like WhatsApp have many desirable uses for the privacy-conscious. They keep user data safe and allow those living in repressive regimes to communicate without being snooped on. The intelligence and law-enforcement agencies have warned that such technologies are also increasingly used by extremists, including ISIS. The Twitter page of the German-language online magazine Kybernetiq was released on social media on December 28, 2015.

Those tracking the usage of encrypted technology by Jihadists say the problem is growing. In recent months, there has been a visible shift by ISIS militants toward using some of these secure platforms, particularly Telegram, to spread propaganda messages over the web.

A source in the anti-ISIS Anonymous subgroup GhostSec said that in the past five days alone there has been a surge in the creation of new jihadi chat rooms in Telegram and the hacktivist group is now tracking nearly 300 chat rooms in various languages. It is felt that their Telegram usage is being overlooked. It is a lot more powerful than anyone realizes.

According to Alex Krasodomski of the *Center for the Analysis of Social Media* at the London-based think-tank Demos, the use of encryption technology by militant groups is not a new phenomenon. It has been part of a long tradition. Al-Qaeda had released its own encryption software in 2007. What is new is the increase in numbers and availability of apps that use encryption software, many of which - like messaging apps Telegram and WhatsApp - can be downloaded for free from the Internet. So it's not surprising that "wannabe jihadists are early adopters" of such technology, says Krasodomski. Notably, Kybernetiq advises would-be militants not to use Al-Qaeda encryption software because it is identified as jihadi affiliated.

The boom in the availability of encrypted communication platforms has raised fears that the use by militants of these technologies could pose a serious threat by allowing them to evade monitoring of their messages by security services. In the wake of the November 13, 2015, Paris attacks, for which ISIS claimed responsibility, there was speculation that the attackers had used encrypted communications for plotting and directing the attacks. Krasodomski points out that despite the initial fears the signs show that the ISIS networks involved in the Paris attacks had used un-encrypted technologies. They used old-fashioned text messaging to communicate. So laying the blame for the attacks at the door of cryptography is not the answer. Nevertheless, encryption is a fact and security services should have the capability and tools under the law to deal with this new reality. It's worth noting that even the authors of Kybernetiq magazine are not convinced that encryption software will make them invulnerable to the security services. They advise that jihadists should write important messages on paper and after use, burn them quickly.

Crescent Revisits Europe

Europe, too, has been badly affected by the ISIS virus. Nearly 3,700 of an estimated 5,000 plus fighters have travelled from just four countries: France, Belgium, Germany and the United Kingdom. French officials say that some 1,800 terrorists have emerged from within their borders including several who reportedly returned to carry out terror attacks in Paris that left 131 dead in November, 2015. It was followed by attacks in Brussels. On the morning of 22 March, 2016, three coordinated bombings were staged in Belgium, two at the airport in Zaventum and one at Maalbeek (Molenbeek) metro station. Another bomb was found unexploded during a search of the airport. The responsibility for the bombings was promptly claimed by ISIS. The three attacks were the deadliest act of terrorism in Belgium's history. The Belgian government declared three days of national mourning.

The increase in terror attacks in Europe shows that efforts to contain the flow of foreign recruits to extremists groups in Syria and Iraq have had very limited impact. In Molenbeek, a notorious neighborhood of Brussels, one can see the soldiers carrying machine guns patrolling the streets. Saleh Abdeslam a surviving participant in the Paris attacks of November, 2015, had taken refuge in this ghettoized epicenter of jihad before his arrest on 18th March, 2016. Another terrorist, Abdelhamid Abaaoud, who is believed to be the ace plotter behind the Paris attacks also lived in Molenbeek. In all 14 Muslims involved in the Paris attacks lived in Brussels.

The Brussels bombings of March, 2016 were the worst incidents of terrorism in the history of Belgium. It may be recalled that Belgium has more nationals fighting for the Islamic State as a proportion of its population, than any other Western Europe country – an estimated 440 Belgians having left for Syria and Iraq till January 2015. Due to Belgium's weak security apparatus and poor intelligence architecture, the country has become a hub of jihadi recruitment and terrorist activities. Even prior to the March 2016 bombings, several terrorist attacks had originated from Belgium. In May 2014, a gunman attacked the Jewish Museum of Belgium killing four persons. In January 2015, the police undertook anti-terrorist operations against a group believed to be planning another *Charlie Hebdo* type shooting in Brussels and Zaventem. The operation led to an encounter in which two jihadi suspects were killed. Again, in August 2015, another suspected terrorist shot and stabbed passengers travelling in a train on its way from Amsterdam to Paris via Brussels. Luckily he was subdued and disarmed by alert American passengers.

Investigations revealed that the perpetrators involved in the November, 2015, attacks in Paris were based in Molenbeek. Consequently Brussels was locked down for five days to allow the police to search for suspects. On 18 March, 2016, Salah Abdsalam, a suspected accomplice in those attacks, was captured after two anti-terrorist raids in Molenbeek that killed another suspect and injured two others. During interrogation, Abdesalam was shown the photographs of the Bakraoui siblings, who later came to be suspected of committing the terror attacks in Brussels three days later. After the attacks in Brussels it took nearly two weeks for the police officials to discover that the conspirators had originally intended to hit Paris again. They did not realize that the two attacks were carried out by a single network. Even now the authorities don't know the full scale of the Islamic State's operations in Europe.

During the last few years, Islamic State operatives have moved freely across the borders of Europe. Investigators now assume that there may be more terrorist cells in countries where violence has yet to occur and Britain, Germany and Italy are believed to be the probable targets. The repetitive audacious attacks by the jihadi groups reinforce the urgent need to fix the problems in Europe's inadequate and flawed security and law enforcement systems.

In the second week of April, 2016, Belgium police arrested one Mohamed Abrini who confessed to being the third man in the Brussels Airport bombing. The arrest, while critically important, was also a reminder of the cross-border nature of the operations. Abrini is believed to have played an important logistical role in staging the Paris attacks in November, 2015.

Cooperation between different police forces of the European Union is also hampered by differences in languages and their assessments about the severity of the terrorist threat. Ever since its inception, the European Union has been more bothered about economic issues than the security paradigm. There is no centralized intelligence service for the European Union. Most European governments rely on the United States for intelligence. They share data with America's Central Intelligence Agency or the Federal Investigation Bureau more than other European nations. After the bombings in Paris and Brussels the need for greater teamwork has become all the more pressing because of Europe's porous borders which once exemplified freedom of movement. But now borderless Europe presents a huge challenge at a time when thousands of Europeans are being recruited by ISIS and refugees from West Asia are flooding Europe.

Barely one month before the Brussels mayhem, the Obama administration sent an expert team to work with the Belgians on strengthening their defenses. Since then, airports in Europe have tightened scrutiny in hiring of airport staff and other security procedures. But ultimately, the prevention of terrorist attacks depend on the implementation of effective security checks. Investigations revealed that the bombers at the Brussels Airport took advantage of lack of a strong and uniform enforcement system.

The increase in jihadi attacks worldwide shows that by now Islamic State has developed spies and agents almost all over the world. They are embedded in sensitive facilities like airports, metro stations and malls. The revelation became public when recently in Canada, a Muslim who had stabbed soldiers was found to have acquired the requisite security clearance to work at an airport. Latest investigations have revealed that US intelligence agencies had found as many as 73 employees with terrorist ties working at forty U.S. airports. A Muslim baggage handler at Minneapolis-St. Paul International Airport boasted of his ability to bring down a plane.[1]

The Islamic State has hundreds of agents working in Western airports, metro stations and very sensitive facilities in the world – claimed leading Islamic State-allied militant in an exclusive interview. Abu al-Ayna al-Ansari, a Salafist senior official in the Gaza Strip, made the claim in a pre-recorded, one hour-long interview for airing in full on Sunday on the *"Aaron Klein Investigative Radio"*, the popular weekend talk radio program.[2] Ansari is a well-known Gazan Salafist, a jihadi allied with Islamic State ideology. During the interview with Klein, Ansari seemed to be speaking as an actual ISIS member repeatedly using the pronoun "we" when referring to the ISIS. Ansari claimed that the Islamic State is a full-fledged State and has agents all over in very sensitive facilities in the world, like metro stations, airports and other places, both in the West and in the Arab world. There are mujahedeen planted in those facilities as workers, as employees, even in the security of airports, he asserted. They were recruited to work for the Islamic State and have succeeded in infiltrating very deep in these facilities. They showed their prowess in Sinai by downing a Russian jet. We are showing it again and again. Everybody should understand this state will not disappear. It will only become bigger. This is the prophecy of Muhammad and this is the promise of Allah, he pronounced.[3] According to reliable estimates, citizens from nearly 100 countries are currently fighting in the ranks of ISIS terrorists. In planting spies and agents across the globe the Military Affiliates called Wilayats of the Islamic State have played a key role. These outposts have added punch and muscle to its underground activities in faraway countries.

The rumblings across the continent indicate that jihadist threat to European Christians will not be controlled easily. On June 14, 2016, a French Muslim of Moroccan origin, Larossi Abballa, stabbed a police officer to death outside his house in Magnanville, a suburb located 60 kms west of Paris. He also killed his partner who worked for the police. The attacker also took the couple's son as hostage during the night of 13th June, 2016, but he was rescued unharmed. Abballa has a history. He was jailed in 2013 for helping some terrorists escape to Pakistan. During interrogation he confessed that he had answered the call given by the Islamic State chief Al Baghdadi to kill the infidels at home, including their families. He also posted a video on the Internet threatening that the Euro football tournament would be reduced to a graveyard. Responding to the growing threat to the Euro-2016 tournament, the Belgian police arrested 12 suspected ISIS moles in the third week of June, 2016.

Attack on Istanbul Airport

ISIS has been merrily going ahead with its bombings and suicide attacks. Istanbul airport was attacked by ISIS on 29 June, 2016, which left 45 people dead and another 49 injured. The suicide bombings shook Turkey as well as the western nations. Among those killed were a number of Europeans. Turkish officials blamed the Islamic State jihadists for their gruesome gun and bomb spree at Ataturk airport. It was one of the deadliest attacks this year on Turkey's biggest city. According to *Agence France-Presse*, thirteen suspects, including ten Turks, have been charged over the Istanbul airport suicide bombings. Officials said that one of the three bombers one was a Russian, one Uzbek and another was a Kyrgyz national. The suspects, who are in police custody, have been charged with murder and endangering the unity of the state.

Turkish media identified Akhmed Chatayev as the organiser of airport attack. Chatayev is a Chechen militant who is believed to head an ISIS cell in Istanbul. He is alleged to have found accommodation for the bombers. Chatayev had allegedly organised two deadly bombings this year in the heart of the city's Sultanahmet tourist district and the busy Istiklal shopping street, the Hurriyet newspaper commented.

Analysts blamed Turkey's President Erdoğan for willful blindness to the threat posed by ISIS. His preference for blaming everything bad that happens in Turkey on the Kurds is no longer acceptable. Turkey has been rocked by a series of attacks in the past one year which were mostly blamed on Kurdish rebels. Quite a few of these are suspected to have been staged by ISIS.

Terror Attack in Nice

On July 14, 2016, the National Day of France, street celebrations in Nice were marred by a jihadi attack which claimed 84 lives including ten children and injuring nearly 200 revelers. A 19-ton truck driven by two Muslim jihadists barreled through the jubilant crowds celebrating the Bastille Day on Promenade des Anglais along the Mediterranean. The attack left behind a two kms long trail of death and destruction. While one of the truck drivers was shot dead, another was captured alive by the police. The truck driver, Mohamed Lahouaie Bouhlel, shot dead by the police, was a Tunisia-born citizen of France.

Jihad in Germany

There seems to be no end to the spate of jihadi attacks across Europe. On 18 July, 2016, a 17 year old Afghan refugee launched an axe attack on commuters travelling in a train which runs between

Treuchlingen and Wuerzburg in Bavaria. The attacker succeeded in inflicting injuries on nearly twenty passengers among whom were four visitors from Hong Kong. At least two train passengers were injured critically. It is alleged that the assailant shouted 'Allah-hu-Akbar' while wielding the axe. The jihadist was shot dead by the police while trying to escape. An ISIS flag was found in the room of the Afghan youth. The ISIS-linked Amaq news agency claimed that the Afghan lad was a fighter for the Islamic State and had carried out the attack while responding to the group's call to target countries fighting the Islamic State. It may be recalled that in May, 2016, a 27 years old Muslim had carried out an attack on a train in southern Germany killing one person and injuring three others. He is now held in a psychiatric hospital.

On the evening of 22 July, 2016, there was an attack on a mall in the Moosach district of Munich in which nine people were reported to have been killed and at least 16 shoppers injured in the shootout. Although there were rumours about the involvement of three unidentified attackers, ultimately the Bavarian police came to the conclusion that the crime was the handiwork of one single terrorist who was a German citizen of Iranian origin. After shooting dead nine people he shot himself presumably to avoid arrest and interrogation by the police. The body of the suspected attacker was found about 1km (0.6 miles) away from the shopping centre. The Bavarian capital's central railway station was evacuated as authorities suspended all public transport. Thousands of people stranded by the emergency were offered shelter by local residents. The initiative was launched with the Twitter hashtag **#Offenetür** (i.e. open door). Preliminary investigations revealed that the attacker was a German citizen of Iranian Origin. His name was Ali.

Again on Sunday 24 July, 2016 there was another bombing in Germany this time in Ansbach, near Nuremburg, in which 12 persons were injured. The attacker was a Syrian asylum seeker who blew himself up – as usual in the cause of Allah the most merciful! The 27 year old youth had been denied access to the nearby Open Musical festival being held in Ansbach. Had the bomber managed to enter the hall the casualties could have been more.

Bombathon During and After Ramdan

Traditionally Ramadan has been regarded as a holy month in the Islamic tradition. As a rule, Muslims abstain from taking food and drink during sunlight hours. A large number of Muslims visit mosques to seek Allah's blessings.

But the history of Islam also tells us that Ramadan is the month for the killing of kaffirs and plundering their lands. The belief that the holy month of Ramadan is a time for war and conquest is deeply embedded in the history of Islam itself. Prophet Muhammad had waged his first offensive jihad through the Battle of Badr during Ramadan in 624 A.D. Later on in the year 630 A.D. he conquered Mecca by waging war during the month of Ramadan, thereby reinforcing the tradition of waging jihad in the holy month of fasting and piety.

It may be recalled that in pre-partition India, the call for jihad given by the Muslim League in August 1946 for the Direct Action Day was rooted in the holy month of Ramadan. A leaflet titled, 'Munajat For Jihad' was circulated by Muhammad Usman, the Mayor of Calcutta (now Kolkata) which heralded the great Calcutta killings. It specifically pointed out that the Prophet had launched the Battle of Badr in the holy month of Ramadan. The handout called upon the faithful to join in the jihad being declared against Hindus in the same month.[4] The proclamation also contained a call for global jihad to establish supremacy of Islam worldwide !

As the holy month approached, Abu Mohammed al-Adnani, the official spokesman of the Caliphate, exhorted the faithful to get ready for making Ramadan a month of calamity and pain for the non-believers everywhere. Responding to the call of ISIS there were a number of bombings worldwide. More than 350 people were killed during a month long bombathon unleashed by ISIS across the globe, ranging from Orlando in USA to Baghdad in Iraq, and onwards to Dhaka in Bangladesh and Istanbul in Turkey. There were ten different attacks which were believed to have been staged worldwide by the Mujahideens of Islamic State in the month of Ramadan and immediately afterwards. Al-Qaeda's official chapter in Syria, the Jabhat-ul Nusra, pompously declared that Ramadan was a month of conquests by the warriors of Islam thereby signaling the Momins to attack and kill the kaffirs. In one single attack in Baghdad on 4th July, 2016, more than 200 people, mostly Shias, were killed.

Growing ISIS Attacks Rile USA

Ever since 9/11 USA has been facing the ire of Islamic militants. The emergence of the Islamic State has added a new dimension to the growing jihadi threat to the USA. According to the Middle East Forum, since 2010 there have been nineteen terrorist attacks on American soil by Islamic outfits, in which 96 persons were killed. It is certain that the Orlando attack is not going to be the last episode of unremitting jihadi violence in the USA. The threat to the lives of innocent citizens is one aspect of the problem. An equally grave issue is the growing fear of violence at the workplace which threatens the business world.

One major terrorist attack which shook the Americans was the shootout in San Bernardino's Inland Regional Center on December, 2015, which left fourteen people dead and 22 injured. A terrorist couple, Rizwan Farook and his wife Afsheen Malik, opened fire at a holiday party at the Inland Regional Center in Bernardino, California. While FBI Director, James Comey, described the couple as "homegrown violent extremists" who had become radicalized over the last few years, the Islamic State claimed the man-and-wife team were their supporters.

Far more shocking however, was the gruesome attack by a lone-wolf gunman Omar Mateen who stormed a gay nightclub in Orlando in Florida State on 12th June, 2016. The jihadi killer armed with an AR-15 assault rifle and a handgun stormed the nightclub 'Pulse' where nearly 300 revelers were having fun. The gunman remained holed up inside the nightclub for nearly two hours with scores of people held hostage, till a SWAT (Special Weapons And Tractics) police team arrived on the scene, killed him and rescued the hostages. Nearly 50 people were killed and another 53 club-goers injured. Omar Mateen was an American citizen of Afghan origin, who, before attacking the nightclub, called 9/11 to declare his allegiance to the Islamic State. Shortly after the shooting rampage, the Amaq news agency representing the ISIS claimed that the shooting was accomplished by one of its fighters. It was the worst terror attack on American soil since September 11, 2001.

The menacing threat to America will not end with these two incidents. Most strategic analysts anticipate many more attacks in the coming months.

ISIS Goes into Overdrive

Islamic State has increased its attacks in Iraq and Syria to the highest level since 2014, according to a report by IHS Janes. The Janes defense think-tank says there were 891 attacks and 2,150 non-militant fatalities recorded in the first three months of last year. The figures represent an increase of 16.7% and 43.9% respectively on the last quarter of 2015. Almost as many attacks took place in the first three months of 2016 as the combined attacks recorded in the third and fourth quarters on 2015. Matthew Henman, Head of *IHS Jane's Terrorism and Insurgency Centre*, said attack and fatality numbers have jumped. Though Henman argues that this increase in attacks shows that the ISIS has come under pressure, his facile reasoning appears to be flawed. The huge increase could be due to a more aggressive campaigning by the ISIS. Lately the jihadi attacks in Libya have intensified after a long slump.

In the month of June there have been two important developments which need mention. First there was news about the death of Al Baghdadi in an airstrike by the U.S. bombers. After spreading some good cheer among the western powers engaged in fighting the ISIS the news about Baghdadi's death got a quiet burial. It was a red herring.

Secondly, there was news that Iraqi troops, supported by American military advisers, managed to enter Fallujah city and capture the main government buildings on 17th June, 2016. The Islamic State has been in control of Falluja city since 2014. The Iraqi government has always viewed Falluja as Islamic State's military stronghold frequently used for suicide attacks in Baghdad. On 23 May, 2016, Operation Break Terrorism was launched by the Iraqi army to free Fallujah from the Islamic State. The operation involved the Iraqi security forces, the Popular Mobilization Units (Shia groups) and local Sunni tribal forces. The operation was supported by US led coalition strikes, that executed several bombings between 14 and 20 May, 2016. In May, 2015 the Iraqi government, supported by Coalition air bombings and Shia militias, launched an attack to free Falluja from ISIS. A large body of Islamic State fighters chose to fight another day by escaping with the fleeing civilians. At long last the 'Operation Break Terrorism' was successful and the Iraqi security forces were able to capture the key town of Fallujah. This was a major setback for Islamic State.

Looking at the size of manpower and high intensity training of tens of thousands of ISIS fighters recruited from around the world, the former Defense Intelligence Agency Director of the USA, Lt-Gen Michael Flynn, warned that soon it might become impossible to defeat them.[5] They have acquired global footprints and were following a global strategy. He admitted that the ISIS have demonstrated an incredible level of resilience and they will not be defeated by military means alone. Equally significant is the observation of Richard Barret, the former head of the Counter Terrorism Cell of MI6 (Britain's Secret Intelligence Service). He confessed that the ISIS cannot be defeated and that the western powers will have to learn to live with it.

Despite masterly assassination of Osama bin Laden in a fortified safe-house of Pakistan by the US Seals in May, 2011, the long march of Islam has continued unchecked – manifestly with greater vigour. Al Baghdadi has emerged an infinitely more dangerous threat to the non-Muslim fraternity than Osama bin Laden ever was. It looks certain that even the elimination of Al Baghdadi will not defeat ISIS!

Islamic State Travels to Brazil

Meanwhile Veryan Khan, Editorial Director of Terrorism Research and Analysis Consortium (TRAC), issued a warning that the Islamic State has now set its eyes on Latin America. To begin with, Brazil has been selected as a soft target for spreading the campaign of global jihad across the south Atlantic, she wrote. A message posted on the ISIS website *Online Dawah Operations* sought the services of male and female volunteers conversant in Spanish and Portuguese. The call was addressed to the 'brothers and sisters' willing to join the translation team for a 'dawah' (conversion to Islam) campaign in Brazil. For creating an Affiliate or Wilayat in South America a former Guantanamo detainee, Jihad Ahmed Mustafa Dhiab, has been deputed to Brazil. A project was launched to organize an effective financing ring and set up a Portuguese-language ISIS-news *Telegram* channel apparently to push forward the *'Dawah'* campaign.

The search for the Spanish and Portuguese speaking Muslims, however, was found to be a part of a conspiracy to attack the Olympic Games 2016 scheduled to be held at Rio de Janeiro in August, 2016. Recent developments confirm that the real purpose of the proposed *'Dawah'* operations in Brazil, by positioning Jihad Ahmed Mustafa in that country, was to target the Olympic Games. The well-known Islam watcher, Donna Bowater, wrote in the London-based newspaper *Telegraph* on 19 July, 2016, that a group of Muslim extremists in Brazil had declared loyalty to the Islamic State. That was barely three weeks before the country hosted the 2016 Olympics. A channel called *"Ansar al-Khilafah Brazil"* by posting a message in app Telegram, pledged allegiance to the ISIS leader Al-Baghdadi, according to the US-based SITE Intelligence Group, which monitors jihadi networks. It is believed to be the first public declaration of becoming an Affiliate of ISIS from an extremist group based in South America.

One message attributed to *'Ansar-al-Khilafah Brazil'* reportedly said that if the French police could not stop attacks on its territory, the training given to the Brazilian police could amount to nothing. The Director of the SITE group and the celebrated author of the book, *Terrorist Hunter*, Rita Katz, pointed out that the timing of the allegiance to Islamic State was "intentional". The "pledge comes shortly before Olympics," she tweeted. Soon thereafter there was a drastic increase in the speed and quality of the western-language ISIS channels (English, Portuguese, Spanish, German, et al) across Brazil. The targeting of Brazil shows that the Islamic State is now on a global expansion spree.

The first alert about the jihadi threat was raised earlier this month when ISIS created a Portuguese channel on *Telegram*, indicating it was aiming to telecast propaganda across Brazil in the run-up to the games. Soon the security services in Brazil started toiling extra hard to reassure the participants and the likely spectators of total security. The security preparations had been ramped up in Rio after the attack in Nice. The fear was palpably noticeable in Rio because an alleged plot against the French Olympic delegation had been foiled by the French police ahead of the games.

By the grace of God, the Olympics went through without any terrorist incident. But for all practical purposes Al Baghdadi has re-confirmed his declaration of war against all kaffirs across the world, ranging from Philippines to Brazil.

CHAPTER 4

Enemy at India's Gate

"Islam was not a religion of peace even for a day"

— Abu Salha al-Hindi, an Indian jihadi who featured
in a video released by ISIS in May, 2016.

No other country in world has such a long, brutal and disastrous encounter with Islam and the blight called 'jihad', as we Indians had for 1200 years. Barely 69 years after independence, once again the monster of global jihad stares us in the face. The Islamic groups have a global vision of establishing a Caliphate covering the entire Indian sub-continent.

Why Jihadis Targets India

The truth behind the repeated targeting of India by multiple jihadi outfits sponsored and nurtured by Pakistan and other hostile nations, has been known for decades to our intelligence agencies, as well as the higher echelons of the government. The most important reason behind the repeated targeting of India is the Islamic doctrine of permanent war against the 'kaffirs'. As already explained, the Pakistani army and the Inter-Services Intelligence (ISI) aided by multiple militant groups, nestling in Pakistan and India, have been waging multiple jihads since 1947 to destroy the Hindu identity of India.

Unfortunately this plain truth has been kept under wraps by our secularism-doped successive governments and secularized politicians for reasons best known to them. Most Indians, including several strategic analysts, foolishly believe that the hostility between the two distant neighbors, India and Pakistan, has been caused by the Kashmir dispute. This frequently trotted politically-correct excuse is nothing but unmitigated falsehood. Many Indians, including the secularists simply refuse to accept the truth that Pakistan and multiple jihadi outfits spawned and supported by it, have been waging a civilizational war against Hindus ever since partition.

Visceral Hatred of Hindus

Even a casual glance at the pronouncements of Pakistani heads of State since Independence and their lackeys in India reveal that they continue to propagate vicious hatred against Hindus. This is vividly reflected in repeated jihadi attacks on India, apart from the publicly practiced persecution of Hindus in Pakistan which led to their near-total ethnic cleansing. In 1947 at the time of partition Hindus and Sikhs constituted nearly 23 percent of the population, but now their percentage is less than 2 in today's Pakistan. There is no end to the woes of the "left over" Hindus and Sikhs in Pakistan. An equally sordid narrative of persecution of Hindus was repeated in Bangladesh which was freed from the jackboot of tyrants by the sacrifices made by Indian soldiers in the 1971 war.

Unfortunately many self-styled intellectuals refuse to learn any lesson from the killings of several lakh Hindus and Sikhs during Partition and the subsequent religious cleansing of Hindus, once again from the Islamized Bangladesh after the 1971 Indo-Pakistan war. They also pretend to forget that barely 26 years ago, in January 1990, a similar pogrom of persecution and ethnic cleansing of Hindus was implemented in the Kashmir Valley.

Immediately after the peace-seeking bus ride of Atal Behari Vajpayee to Lahore in 1999, General Musharraf had told a Karachi audience that the Lahore Declaration of Vajpayee and Pakistan's Prime Minister Nawaz Sharif was nothing but 'hot air' and that low intensity conflict with India would continue even if the Kashmir issue was resolved.[1]

In a similar statement, the true intentions of Pakistan were spelt out by General Aziz Khan, who was Musharraf's closest accomplice in the Kargil war. He made the following candid pronouncement on June 23, 2003, at Rawalkot in Pak-Occupied Kashmir[2]:

"India's religious and economic values are such that Muslims cannot adhere to these. So even if Kashmir issue is resolved we cannot become intimate friends."

But the myopic Indian leadership has persistenly refused to learn any lessons from the blunt pronouncements of Pakistani leaders ! A casual glance at the politico-communal developments across India reveals the contours of the fast-growing multiple jihadi campaigns waiting to erupt in several parts of our motherland. Without mincing words, let me place on record that top intelligence agencies like the Intelligence Bureau and the Research & Analysis Wing of the Cabinet Secretariat, including the top political echelons of the Indian government, are fully aware that the Inter-Services Intelligence of Pakistan, acting in cahoots with multiple Islamic outfits, have drawn up a long term plan to overrun India and kill or convert its Hindu population for establishing a Caliphate in the sub-continent. Their objective is to make India a part of the trans-Asian Caliphate extending from the Philippines via Indonesia and India to the demographically-dying Christian Europe in the west. The latest threat to India, however, comes from ISIS which has become the world's most successful terrorist group of Islam.

According to Sarah A. Carter of the American Media Institute (AMI), a recruitment document of the Islamic State found in June-July, 2015, in Pakistan's lawless tribal region revealed that the extremist group had prepared an ambitious plan for organizing a new terrorist army in Afghanistan and Pakistan for mounting an attack on India by triggering a war to provoke an Armageddon-like "end of the world" scenario.[3] The original report in Urdu language was a 32 page document which was procured by the American Media Institute (AMI) and analyzed by the strategic journal, USA Today. The document was titled, *"A Brief History of the Islamic State Caliphate (I. S. C.), a Caliphate according to The Prophet"*. It detailed a plot to attack U S soldiers as and when they withdraw from Afghanistan and then target American diplomats and Pakistani officials, too. The analysts who verified the document from different angles held that the document was authentic. There are, however, some experts who have questioned the reliability of the document. But at least three strategic experts have confirmed that it is authentic.

The grand strategy of the ISIS is to unite all factions of the Pakistani and Afghan Taliban into a single army of terrorists to target India. According to the American Media Institute the proposed onslaught presents a never-seen-before chilling battle plan for the coming years. The document further emphasizes that the leader of the Islamic State should be recognized as the sole ruler of the world's one billion Muslims under a religious empire called the "caliphate". It may be recalled that Abu Bakr al-Baghdadi had laid claim to be recognized as leader of the global Ummah when he announced the formation of the caliphate on 29th June, 2014. The ISIS further ordered all Muslims, including the Al Qaeda, to accept the fact that this Caliphate would survive and prosper until it took over the entire world and beheaded every last person who rebelled against Allah. It proclaimed: "This is the bitter truth, swallow it". In November, 2014, Al-Baghdadi demanded that jihadi movements across the world must be dissolved and their members absorbed into the armed forces of his 'Caliphate'. Several Islamic groups responded positively to the call. There are signs that many new Islamic outfits will also do so. The appeal of revitalising the Caliphate is sure to win the allegiance of many more extremist groups. Equipped with state-of-the-art armaments and the latest American war hardware seized from defeated Iraqi troops, the ISIS is now well entrenched in West Asia and parts of Africa. It will not be easy to defeat the ISIS unless thousands of boots of battle-hardened combatants are placed on the ground. American soldiers, supported by air attacks, will not be able to defeat them easily. To date, no western power has dared to send ground troops to fight the Islamic State. It is felt that the combat manpower required for ground operations will be huge.

Regardless of the doubts about the authenticity of the document found and analyzed by the American Media Institute, the threat of ISIS to India remains daunting. The real danger to India comes from the group's rabid fanaticism and appeal to all Muslims living beyond the borders of Iraq, Syria and Afghanistan to join its global jihad and the repeated threats to India issued by Baghdadi. Al-Baghdadi has assumed the title of "the Commander of the Faithful" and claims to exercise the ecclesiastical authority vested in caliphs from the earliest days of Islam. This along with extensive use of social media has proved to be a powerful magnet for drawing young jihadists from India and several parts of the world into joining the Islamic State.

Junod-al Khalifa al Hind

Islamic State has set up an India-specific outfit called Junod-al Khalifah-al Hind for speeding up recruitment of Indian youth for jihad. One Rizwan Ahmed alias Khalid was appointed as the second-in command of the radical group, Junod-al Khalifa-Hind (Army of Caliph of India). The outfit is affiliated to Islamic State. The 20 year old Rizwan Ahmed was arrested before Republic Day in the fourth week of January, 2016. He belongs to Kushi Nagar in Uttar Pradesh and was reported to be in touch with the Caliphate-based Yusuf Al-Hindi which is code name for Shafi Armar, the alleged co-founder of the Indian arm of Islamic State.

In a series of raids across the country before the Republic Day 2016, the National Investigation Agency arrested fourteen suspected moles including Rizwan Ahmed and a Maharashtra-based mole, Mudabbir Mushtaq Shaikh. The group had reportedly started receiving money through 'hawala' route. One of the accused was alleged to have received a sum of Rs. 6 lakh from abroad, ostensibly for launching terrorist attacks in Indian cities. ISIS is reported to have issued a 'Kill List' of more than 5,000 persons, mostly American citizens, whom they want to assassinate through lone-wolf attacks. It is alleged that among them there are names of 285 Indians who are yet to be identified by Indian intelligence agencies.

The investigations conducted by the National Investigation Agency (NIA) into an ISIS case relating to India, show how Karnataka has become central to the conspiracy. Out of the nine crucial meetings that the alleged operatives held, five were in Karnataka, the NIA states. It was further learnt that the meetings in Karnataka were held on a regular basis where a conspiracy was hatched not just to recruit more youth and establish a Caliphate in India, but also to carry out attacks in various parts of the country. The National Investigation Agency (NIA) had on December 9, 2015 arrested 18 people from across the country after it had been found that they were part of an Indian ISIS module. However two were granted conditional pardon by the court following which a charge sheet against the rest was filed. Apart from the meetings that were held in Karnataka, the NIA also states that the driving force behind this module was Shafi Armar from Bhatkal. Shafi and his brother Sultan had started the Ansar-ul-Tawhid, a recruiting wing for the ISIS in India. However with the heat building up on the outfit they changed the name to Junod ul-Khilafa-Hind. The meetings in Karnataka that the alleged operatives had were held at Devarayana Dargah, state forest Tumkur, in the month of August, 2015. The second meeting was held at Deoband in September, 2015. This was followed by another meeting at Tumkur hills in October, 2015. The fourth and fifth meeting were held at the residences of two accused persons Suhail and Afzal at Bengaluru on October 24th and 25th, 2015 respectively. The rest of the meetings were held in Lucknow on November 1, 2015, Hyderabad on December 14, 2015 and Pune on December 18, 2015. The last meeting was at Pune.

Project Wilayat Hind

A well-known ISIS watcher, Carol Grayson (also known as 'Radical Sister'), has pointed out in her blog, that the ISIS has now set its sights on the creation of Wilayat Hind. This development should be a cause of serious concern to India. In the second week of January, 2016, ISIS had put out the following statement reiterating their goal of targeting India in bad English:

"The Islamic State of Khorasan is increasing and strengthening day by day Alhamdulillah's, but still not progress like our Core Areas like Iraq Libya, Egypt and Syria there we have full strength and fully equipped, but many individuals and groups are joining IS-Khurasan day by day and inshallah after few months or may be a year, you will hear about IS Wilayat-e-Hind inshallah, and inshallah this good news will be coming from Punjab and Sindh Areas because Sind and Punjab and India. The Islamic state

*declared a Map and shows these areas in Wilayat-e-Hind and
yes there in the news we see many Newspapers and T.V.
channels called ISIS is fighting with Al Qaeda and Taliban
it's true, but not with all Taliban and Al Qaeda but only few,
because many groups are still silent and many are pledging
allegiance with ISIS, of course Islamic State Khurasan
brothers are belong to Afghan and Pak majority. Yes, few
groups like the Mullah Akhter group are fighting with ISIS
Khurasan, only with the help of local militias and Afghan
NDS and Pakistani Agencies.*[4]

A map showing the States of India proposed to be included in
Wilayat-e Hind was also issued by ISIS.[5]

ISIS in West Bengal & Bangladesh

It was highlighted by Abhinandan Mishra in an article published in
The Sunday Guardian on October 11, 2015, that some supporters of
the Islamic State (ISIS) have been putting up posters in several
districts of West Bengal exhorting the youth to join the terrorist
organization. Earlier Intelligence Bureau had warned the Ministry of
Home Affairs that the West Bengal government were yet to wake up
to the danger of the ISIS which has found an operationally active
foothold in the State. They expressed concern that the Trinamool
Congress government was not doing enough to control the radical
elements in the state. According to reliable sources many Muslim
youth of Murshidabad and Nadia districts in West Bengal have
developed fascination for ISIS. Posters exhorting the youth to join
ISIS and contribute to the 'Islamic cause' have been found in many
parts of the two districts. According to an Intelligence Bureau officer
the state government needs to do more to curb the radicalized activists
promoting the ISIS ideology in the State. It seems that the state

government continues to be reluctant to act tough against the ISIS supporters, a large number of whom are illegal immigrants. Muslims constitute nearly 27 percent of West Bengal's population. They had been traditionally voting *en bloc* for the leftists since the late 1970s. But in the 2014 general elections they switched loyalties to the Trinamool Congress because of which the party won 34 out of the 42 Lok Sabha seats in West Bengal. Intelligence officials suspect that activists of Jamaat-ul-Mujahideen Bangladesh, which has a strong network in West Bengal were helping the recruiters of the Islamic State. The officials monitoring the growing use of social media by the ISIS supporters in West Bengal have conveyed their worries to the Central Government. There has been a shift in the emphasis on the methodology of action. Now ISIS handlers have started asking their supporters to launch jihad from wherever they happen to be located, instead of proceeding to the war zones of Syria or Afghanistan. The youth, including some girls, mostly in the age group of sixteen to thirty years, are being asked to start the holy war from their places of residence. They are being told that there is no need for them to go to Syria to join the war. They could fight against the infidels right here in India.

In recent months Islamic State has been claiming that they have established strong presence from Bangladesh to Tunisia and beyond. The outfit has also owned responsibility for the killings of many secular bloggers in Bangladesh. The following prominent intellectuals and human rights activists were killed by the jihadists claiming to be affiliated either to the Islamic State or Al-Qaeda during the last two years:

1. *Cesare Tavella* – An Italian aid worker
2. *Sadhu Paramananda Roy* – A Hindu priest and preacher
3. *Kunio Hoshi* – A Buddhist Shrine Project Manager
4. *Niloy Neel* – A secular blogger
5. *Oyasiqur Rahman Babu* – An atheist critic of religion

6. *Hussein Ali Sarkar* – A convert to Christianity
7. *Shafiul Islam* – A Professor and advocate of secularism
8. *Jogeshwar Dasadhikari* – A Hindu priest
9. *Nazimuddin Samad* – A liberal blogger
10. *Ananta Bijoy Das* – A blogger writing on science and logic
11. *Xulhaz Mannan* – A gay rights magazine editor
12. *Faisal Arefin Dipan* – A secular book publisher
13. *Tanay Majumder* – An actor suspected to be homosexual
14. *Rezaul Karim Siddique* – A Professor and music lover
15. *Avijit Roy* – An atheist author
16. Nikhil Joarder – A Hindu tailor

This is a brief list of some of the outspoken activists killed by the militant operatives of ISIS. The total number of writers and intellectuals killed is said to be around 150. More than forty of them were Hindus.

Though the Bangladesh government keeps denying the claims made by the ISIS about its growing clout across the country, an analysis of the latest developments reveals that the ground situation is quite serious as indicated below:

- The ISIS is no longer a Middle East based phenomenon. It has reached our backyard in Bangladesh. Over the last few decades, a phenomenal societal change has come over in Bangladesh. This inevitably follows from the flow of Wahhabi money.

- Bangladesh is a convenient small state with no apparent geopolitical issues attracting attention, and hence can be a convenient haven for jihadi outfits to park themselves away from international glare.

- According to knowledgeable analysts the ISIS, has infiltrated the very core of Bangladesh in recent times. It is clear from the fact that the Hizb-utTahrir sponsored website has been receiving a record number of hits. The indoctrinated clients are not the usual semi-educated madrassa folks any more. A majority of them belong to the sophisticated urban middle class, including university educated youth and professionals in the country's huge diaspora spread across the globe.

- When secular blogger Abhijit was murdered (the first blogger in the series), there was a huge surge of posts on the social media, applauding the horrendous killing. Emphatic endorsements followed the next blogger's murder.

- The indoctrination has also been targeting the armed forces and police personnel. Every day there are new posters or new Facebook pages with a battle cry against India and of course, the USA, too.

- By the time the authorities remove one offending post another one springs up. The ISIS in Bangladesh is not only about rhetoric and slitting the throats of kaffirs and bloggers, it is very well organized and deeply entrenched. According to informed sources nearly 150 critics of radical Islam have been murdered so far and another 1200 injured. An LeT bomb-maker "Bomaru Nizam" having connections with the Indian Mujahideen, was arrested by the security forces. He was forcibly rescued in a daring raid by hardcore militants. Each ISIS module operates on its own and no captured terrorist knows anything about the plans of the parent organization. The number of ISIS modules in Bangladesh is fairly large almost uncountable. According to reliable sources the Bangladesh authorities have estimated that there are nearly 60 terror modules and sleeper cells located in the neighboring Indian State of West Bengal as well. They constitute a potential threat to peace in the two neighbouring countries. It is a fact that if those chance bomb blasts had not occurred in October-November, 2014, in Burdwan district, the Indian sleuths could not have known much about the bomb making facilities created in Bengal.

- India has a 4,500 Kms. long border with Bangladesh most of which is inadequately protected. Much of the population along the border on both sides happen to be Sunni-Muslims commanded by radical Imams. A sample of enforcement of Sharia law was lucidly demonstrated when the village Imam banned a women's football match on the Indian soil in West Bengal.

- It is necessary to keep track of the fallout in West Bengal and adjoining States of political developments in Bangladesh. For knowing how things evolved one has to look at the growth of Hizb-ut-Tahrir in Bangladesh. The outfit was founded in 1953 as a Sunni Muslim organization in Jerusalem by Taqiuddin al-Nabhani, an Islamic scholar and Judge (Qadi) from the Palestinian village of Ijzim. The well-known Islamic ideologue Omar Bakri Mohammad, who had studied in Cairo's prestigious Al Azhar University, was able to set up a branch of Hizb-ut-Tahrir in the United Kingdom in 1986, after his expulsion from Saudi Arabia. Since then Hizb ut-Tahrir has spread to more than 50 countries, including Bangladesh. According to one estimate it has about one million members worldwide. The Bangladesh government had recognized its radical threat and banned Hizb ut-Tahrir in October, 2009, for destabilizing the country. The then Home Minister of Bangladesh, Sahira Khatoon, had told the AFP that Hizb ut Tahrir Bangladesh was being banned for violating the laws of the land. But all this has not stopped the ISIS from including Bangladesh in their cascading arc of Islamic terror in South Asia.

In April, 2016, the Islamic State formally announced it plan to target and massacre the Hindus of Bangladesh. After a series of attacks on non-Muslims since last year, including the killings of foreign nationals, Hindu priests and several intellectuals, the Islamic State formally accepted allegiance from a group of local jihadis of Bangladesh. The group known as Jamaat-ul Mujahideen Bangladesh

(JMB) was declared to be an ally of ISIS. The porous border of Bengal, divided by riverine enclaves could well be the stepping stone for the extremist group to launch jihadi operations in this sensitive part of the country. Bangladesh is being promoted as the new hunting ground by JMB and Islamic State in the South Asia region for its militant activities and as an important base from where it can launch its attacks in India.

Islamic State's mouthpiece journal, Dabiq, released online on 13th April, 2016, declared that the Islamic State had appointed a new Emir of Bengal and highlighted its plans to enforce Sharia in Bangladesh and India. In an interview published in the magazine, Sheikh Abu Ibrahim al-Hanafi (real identity unknown) was introduced as the Emir (chief leader) of Soldiers of Khilafah in Bengal. Abu Ibrahim promptly vowed to banish the deviant and apostate sects in Bengal in order to bring Bangladesh into the fold of Islamic State's version of puritanical Islam. The Soldiers of Khilafa group intends to make use of the strategic geographical location of Bangladesh for launching jihadi operations in India. They intend to target Burma (Myanamar), too. Having a strong jihad base in Bangladesh will facilitate guerilla attacks inside India from both sides. It will further facilitate creation of the condition of tawahhush (conflict) in India with the help of the existing local mujahideen there, according to Abu Ibrahim. He blamed the Bengali Muslims for deviating from the 'true understanding of the Sala' (the original followers of Prophet Mohammad in the seventh century) and blamed the local political parties of pining for secular democracy instead of Islamic rule in Bangladesh. The neighboring India and its majority Hindu population are seen by the ISIS as enemies of Islam and an obstruction to the extension of the Caliphate.

Abu Ibrahim announced that the local government led by Prime Minister Sheikh Hasina was an ally of India. It has been supporting the Indian intelligence agency (RAW) to target Islamic groups and

Muslims in Bangladesh since country's liberation in 1971. "Thus, we believe sharia in Bengal won't be achieved until the local Hindus are targeted in mass numbers and until a state of polarization is created in the region, dividing between the believers and the disbelievers," asserted Abu Ibrahim.

Among those targeted in a series of beheadings and killings in Bangladesh by ISIS since last year, were nearly 40 Hindus, several Christians, a number of Muslim agnostics and a few foreign nationals. Authorities in Bangladesh have been repeatedly dismissing the claims of violent attacks as the handiwork of ISIS. But recently the truth came out in open. After a series of attacks by ISIS lone-wolves the Bangladesh government was forced to act and arrest nearly 11,000 suspected Islamic militants. Police investigations and subsequent arrests in the attacks claimed by ISIS have been traced to local jihadi group the Jamaat-ul Mujahideen Bangladesh (JMB) which is believed to be aligned with Islamic State.

Abu Ibrahim admitted that his followers who have pledged allegiance to the Islamic State were small in number and possessed limited means for launching regular military operations. But he affirmed that ISIS branch in Bangladesh has the ability to communicate and coordinate with their base in Wilayat Khorasan. He also assured that the interests of Rohingyas in Burma, oppressed by the majority Buddhist population, will also be looked after when the group extends its capabilities beyond Bengal. It is, however, not clear whether Sheikh Abu Ibrahim is a member of the Jamaat'ul Mujahideen Bangladesh. But he owes allegiance to the Islamic State.

ISIS Dials Dhaka

On the night of July 1, 2016, ISIS hit Dhaka, the capital of Bangladesh, with a bang. A group of nine militants shouting 'Allahu Akbar' meaning "God is great", burst into the Holey Artisan Bakery at 9.20 pm local time on Friday night. In the beginning of the siege, after the fidayeens forcibly barged into the Café, a posse of policemen tried to enter the premises. But they could not because they were showered with a hail of bullets and grenades.

The assailants held about 35 diners as hostages and exchanged sporadic gunfire with police and the security forces for nearly 11 hours. All efforts of the authorities to negotiate with the jihadists for getting the hostages released failed. The army was called out to deal with the crisis and tanks were out in the streets.

After the security forces stormed into the Café, six ISIS militants were killed, one was captured alive while two managed to escape. During the long siege the jihadists had massacred 22 persons including 2 policemen. After military operations 13 hostages were freed. An eye witness, Reazaul Karim, told Bangladesh's widely read newspaper, *Daily Star,* that the gunmen were doing a background check on the religion of hostages by asking everyone to recite verses from the Quran. Those who could recite a verse or two were spared. The others were tortured and killed. Army Brigadier General Nayeem Ashfaq Chowdhury said most of the hostages were killed mercilessly by sharp weapons. But local reports of beheadings of hostages remained unconfirmed. Among those killed were nine Italians and seven Japanese. An Indian teenager Tarushi Jain, 19, was also among those killed. The Prime Minister of Bangladesh, Sheikh Hasina Wajid, vowed to fight terrorism and urged people to come forward with information about terrorists. The most disturbing aspect of the Dhaka Café attack was its religion-specific dimension. The hostages were put through an Islamic test. Those who could recite the verses from Quran were asked to have their food and then allowed to go home. All non-Muslims, including those Muslims who could not recite Ayats were herded together, tortured and then killed by slitting their throats. All attackers, excepting one, were well educated young Bangladeshi Muslims coming from decent background. At least two of them had studied in foreign universities. In a nutshell the killer squad consisted entirely of home-grow terrorists whose modus operandi was the same as that of the ISIS operatives.

The attack on the Dhaka Café did not come as a major surprise to strategic analysts. It only marked an escalation in the two years long spell of frequent atrocities on non-Muslims by Islamic militants strutting across Bangladesh.

Deceptive Infiltration Into West Bengal

Another disturbing development is the enhanced threat posed by the infiltration of ISIS modules from Bangladesh into West Bengal. The Jamaat-ul Mujahedeen Bangladesh (JMB) is now trying to unleash mayhem in West Bengal by deploying its operatives to recreate the 'Orlando Massacre' scenarios in many Hindu populated areas of West Bengal. According to a dispatch appearing on 17th June, 2016, in Bengali newspaper Jugosankha many JMB operatives were entering West Bengal by availing the Medical Tourism package. They cross the border by travelling in Maitree Express or Dhaka-Kolkata bus service and stay in various Muslim owned Multi Specialty hospitals and Nursing Homes in and around Kolkata disguised as patients. Their ultimate objective is to form modules of Islamic militants. These revelations came to light from a leaked intelligence report. An Intelligence Bureau alert warned that a network for the purpose has been established in Kolkata. It is suspected that many such 'Jihadi patients' might not return to Bangladesh at all and stay underground in Muslim populated areas. According to unconfirmed reports many Jihadi sleeper cells have come up in Park Circus, Kiderpur, Rajabazar, Mominpur, Metiaburz, Kalutola in Kolkata and districts of Murshidanad, Nadia, South and North 24 Parganas, Uttar Dinajpur, Malda, Howrah and border areas of West Bengal.

The serial Khagragarh blasts of 2014 in Burdwan district revealed the dangerous face of Jamaat-ul Mujahideen Bangladesh (JMB) in West Bengal. The outfit has been under the scanner of the National Investigation Agency (NIA) since October, 2014. The latest report of the National Investigating Agency reveals that the two radical outfits, the JMB and Ansarullah Bangla, of Bangladesh are mainly controlled by Islamic State. They are now trying to spread ISIS activism in West Bengal by recruiting Muslim youth. In this context the new mission is 'Target Bangla' to strike in Orlando style.

Dabiq also profiled Abu Jandal al-Bangali, another young Muslim from Dhaka who died fighting in Syria. The ISIS mouthpiece claimed that Abu Jandal belonged to a well-to-do military family and his father had fought against Pakistan to liberate Bangladesh.

Ramakrishna Mission Threatened

The ISIS has served a notice on monks of Ramakrishna Mission by ordering them to get out of Bangladesh or face death. Swami Sevananda, the monk in charge of Dhaka Ramakrishna Mission has received a death threat from one A.B. Siddiqui who claims to be an activist of Islamic State. The threat received on June 8, 2016, came in the form of a letter following a series of murders across the country by militants claiming to represent ISIS. It warned Swami Sevananda not to preach his religion through Ramakrishna Mission in an Islamic state like Bangladesh. The priest was told in the letter that Bangladesh being an Islamic State, Hindus can't preach their religion in that country. If the monks continued to preach the Hindu faith, he and others in the monastery would be hacked to death with machetes. The year of the threatened killings was not mentioned, but it is presumed to be the current year. Earlier in January, 2016, another monk of Ramakrishna Mission was threatened by the members of *Ansarullah Bahini* which is believed to be a group associated with the ISIS.

Ramakrishna Mission is a well-known monastic order established and blessed by Swami Vivekananda.

The latest developments in Bangladesh are more horrific. Almost all Hindu priests and monks are living in great panic after receiving death threats from the JMB and ISIS modules sprawling all over Bangladesh. It is learnt that during the first two weeks of July, 2016, at least 15 temple priests and Hindu and Buddhist Monks received letters threatening to kill them unless they quit Bangladesh. According to informed sources during the first six months of the current year (Jan-June, 2016), six Hindu priests were hacked to death by suspected Islamic militants. For all practical purposes a grand project of killing Hindu priests has been launched by Islamic outfits of Bangladesh.

The wave of targeted killings by the activists of Islamic State has created tremendous fear among Hindus who have been warned that Bangladesh is a country exclusively meant for Muslims. This has forced the Hindus to form a self-protection group, Jaatiya Hindu Mahajote, which has demanded that the government provide enhanced security to the beleaguered minority. In an article published on 24th June, 2016, in *Indian Express*, New Delhi, Syed Badrul Ahsan claimed that the degree of fear raging in Bangladesh was so high, that in many areas Hindus prefer to stay indoors. As a safety precaution many Hindu women have taken to wearing the Muslim attire called burka or veil. *'Run Hindu, run!'* has become the battle cry of Islamic fundamentalists of Bangladesh.

Unfortunately the ruling Awami League Government in Bangladesh has failed to save the lives of the members of the minorities in Bangladesh. Several months ago advisories were issued by the governments of America and United Kingdom alerting their citizens to remain extra vigilant during their visits to Bangladesh. Now the chicken have come home to roost!

According to reliable information ISIS and its associated radical groups have started directing the Muslims of Bangladesh and West Bengal to carry out targeted 'lone-wolf' attacks because such attacks are difficult to prevent. Apart from West Bengal, attempts are being made in Jammu and Kashmir, Maharashtra, Uttar Pradesh and Assam, to attract more youth into joining the war against infidels, so that an affiliate Caliphate can be established in India.

Visit of Wahabi Preachers To India

It was pointed out in an article posted on Yale Global Online by Saroj Kumar Rath (who teaches in Delhi University and is the author of the book, *Fragile Frontiers*) that after the NATO withdraws from Afghanistan, the jihadists will eye India. Pakistan regards India as its topmost enemy and some officials even encourage terrorists to target areas like Kashmir and Mumbai.

Prof. Rath further pointed out, that in a classified note India's Intelligence Bureau had highlighted that in the year 2013 nearly 25,000 Wahhabi scholar from twenty countries had gone around eight Indian states, namely Uttar Pradesh, Rajasthan, Chhattisgarh, Andhra Pradesh, Kerala, Bihar, Maharashtra and Jharkhand and addressed nearly twelve lakh 1.2 million Muslims, preaching to them the hard-liner Islamic doctrine. These radical preachers had visited 7,000 registered madrasas in India. Presumably their goal was to motivate youth for waging jihad against kaffir Hindus and ensure implementation of the sharia law in India. The hidden agenda of the visiting Imams could be to prepare these institutions as potential sources for the recruitment and grooming of Muslim youth to join the ranks of Al Qaeda, ISIS, Indian Mujahideen, etc. The support of India's 'Muslims first' Prime Minister, Dr. Manmohan Singh, for allowing 25,000 foreign Ulemas to move and preach all over India has been questioned by many sources.[6] Surprisingly this information, available in the public domain and reiterated by Prof. Rath has not been officially confirmed. But, more important is the fact that it has not been denied either. Meanwhile extremist groups like Al Qaeda, Indian Mujahideen and ISIS have been working overtime to increase their influence in India, wherever necessary, by doling out money to young men.

Prof. Rath warns that the jihadi threat to India posed by the combined efforts of the Islamic State, Al Qaeda and Pakistan is likely to increase in the coming years. The proposed drawdown from Afghanistan by the North Atlantic Treaty Organization and the rapid rise of the Islamic State has made India more vulnerable to terrorist attacks. The Indian nation is dangerously surrounded by multiple jihadi threats from Al Qaeda; the Islamic State (also known as IS, ISIS or ISIL) and the Haqqani network. All terrorist threats in South Asian countries are linked, wrote Prof. Rath. If suppressed at one place in India, they break out in another location. Rogue jihadi groups continue to wander from the frontlines in Kashmir to the sidelines in Afghanistan or Iraq. Prof. Rath has analyzed the following specific trends which underline the increased threat to India.

- In Afghanistan, nearly 87,000 troops of North Atlantic Treaty Organization (NATO) fighting the Islamic insurgents are due to retreat in the near future. Thereafter the United States will leave behind only 10,000 trainers, as per the US-Afghan Bilateral Security Agreement. While NATO troops are preparing to withdraw without winning the 13-years long war, the Al Qaeda, Taliban and their Pakistani associates have started proclaiming victory. The rising number of assaults repeatedly staged in Afghanistan, signal that the balance of power is tilting in favor of militant groups. For the present the proposed withdrawal from Afghanistan appears to have been put on hold.

- As and when the NATO troops withdraw, anti-India elements in Pakistan will direct militants to plan focused jihad against India. The Islamic State, as warned by J.N. Choudhury, Director General of India's National Security Guards, is the latest and the most lethal Islamic entity which is likely to encourage multi-city attacks across India.

- India's contemporary terrorist threat reflects a likely repeat of our recent history. Let us not forget that in 1989 Pakistan's Inter-Services Intelligence came out triumphant after their victory in Afghanistan and stepped up the guerrilla warfare in Kashmir. India was caught napping and Kashmir was plunged into a mammoth militancy which culminated in the ethnic cleansing of nearly four lakh Hindus from the valley.

- Anti-India forces embedded in the Pakistan Army have been trying to shift the focus of terrorist groups from the AFPAK region to India. According to a reliable source, the Lashkar has already joined hands with the ISIS. NATO's withdrawal from Afghanistan will render hordes of Af-Pak jihadists jobless. Apparently this process has already started. The Haqqani network is collaborating with the Lashkar to hit Indian interests in Afghanistan and Kashmir. The appointment of Farman Shinwari, a Landi Kotal based militant and old Kashmir hand, as the chief of Al Qaeda in Pakistan, has added more grist to the jihadi mill. As confirmed by the Srinagar-based commander of India's 15 Corps, Kashmiri youth have been hitting the streets carrying the ISIS flags.

Prof. Rath urges the Indian government to undertake comprehensive profiling of all suspected militants and devise a mechanism for seamlessly scrutinizing all social media sites to identify the sources of jihadi indoctrination. There should be a system for countering all such websites and internet posts.[7]

Besides Al Qaeda, the Haqqani network and ISIS, India continues to face threats from Pakistani militants trained to infiltrate India. The US presence in Afghanistan has, to some extent, countered the inflow of Islamic terrorism into India. Once this protection disappears, India will again be exposed to multiple asymmetrical terrorist attacks. In December 2012, the former Tehrik-e-Taliban Pakistan chief, Hakimullah Mehsud, had demanded that the Pakistan army stop fighting against Afghan insurgents and refocus on the war of revenge against India. Such demands are likely to materialize openly once the NATO troops vacate Afghanistan.[8]

Another noticeable trend is the alleged inter-organizational competition between Al Qaeda and ISIS to enhance their influence and enlist support of disgruntled Indian Muslims who have been choreographed by Pakistan. In 2006, for the first time Osama bin Laden spoke of the Kashmir militancy as a "Zionist-Hindu war against Muslims." Since 2001 many Indian youth have been enticed into joining jihad. They were trained for the holy war in the trenches of the Federally Administered Tribal Areas in Pakistan and in Afghanistan, where they were introduced to the dangerous ideology of Al Qaeda and Taliban. Before their fraternal relationships could fully develop, bin Laden was killed by the USA. Soon afterward, the ISIS was carved out of Al Qaeda by the disgruntled and impatient jihadists of militant groups including the Al-Qaeda and Taliban, and concerted attempts to recruit Indian Muslims were started. There is however a viewpoint that the rivalry between the ISIS and Al Qaeda is being over-emphasized by analysts. The goal of the two organization remains the same, namely to subjugate and annihilate Hindu-dominated India.

A conservative assessment made by Prof. Rath indicated that near about twenty five Indian youth had responded to ISIS chief Abu Bakr al-Baghdadi's call. But the available evidence points to this being a gross underestimate. The National Investigation Agency has already arrested 55 Muslims working for Islamic State. It is believed that post-2016, Afghanistan will become a major launching pad of international terrorism. The jihadis are likely to start a campaign of virulent violence by creating and multiplying pockets of vexation and exhaustion in India. The well-known strategic analyst, M. D. Nalapat, places the number of Indians who joined the ISIS till one year ago in 2015, at about one thousand.

Among other things, Prof. Rath recommends that the Indian government should adopt a two-pronged policy to meet the threat. The first strategy should be to pre-empt and counter the terrorists and their recruiters by profiling the existing and potential militants – by creating a dedicated national anti-terror workforce and integrating inputs from strategic academia in policymaking. The second step should be to work on social sites to check the onslaught of Wahhabi indoctrination. Attempts should also be made to remove the Muslim ghettoization, modernize madrassa education, and support small-scale entrepreneurship among semi-skilled illiterate Muslims, along with other Indian citizens.

We must remember that in September 2014, Al Qaeda had refocussed its attention on India, by opening a branch called Qaedat al-Jihad in the state of West Bengal. Soon thereafter, there were a number of bomb blasts in the border districts of the State. With considerable effort the National Investigation Team was able to control the activities of Al-Qaedat al-Jihad which threatened peace in West Bengal. But the hold of the Qaedat al-Jihad among Muslims of West Bengal and Bangladesh has remained undiluted.

ISIS Modules Embedded in Delhi

With the arrest of five pro-ISIS persons in the second week of January, 2016, including two Bangladeshi nationals, the Delhi Police unearthed an international syndicate involved in facilitating Rohingya

Muslims and Bangladesh nationals to travel to Middle East countries to join the ISIS in Syria.[9] The arrested recruiters were identified as Shaukat Ali and Suleman, both Bangladeshi nationals. Also arrested were three Indian nationals – Saddam Hussain, Ibn-e Sultan and Amit Bodh Jha. According to Delhi police, so far this module has sent nearly 500 Rohingya Muslims to Syria and Iraq to fight for the terror outfit ISIS. According to Special Commissioner of Police, Sundari Nanda, this module was active for the last two years and every month around 20 to 25 Rohingya Muslims were sent to the Middle Eastern countries by paying Rs. two lakhs to each volunteer.

In a joint operation carried out by the police of West Bengal and Hyderabad and overseen by the Central Intelligence agencies, the Delhi police arrested five suspected ISIS supporters in January, 2016. Ms. Sundari Nanda disclosed that efforts were on for tracing another 25 suspected operators. The Anti-Terrorist Cell had received information that a syndicate of Bangladeshi nationals had been active in Delhi to facilitate the procurement of Indian passports and visas for Rohingya Muslims and Bangladeshi nationals to enable them to proceed to countries in the Middle East. One Shaukat Ali, a Bangladeshi national, who was an active member of this syndicate operating from South Delhi, had been acting as the kingpin of the module in Delhi. In addition, the syndicate had modules embedded in Kolkata, Hyderabad and Bangladesh.

Shaukat Ali was in touch with Noor-ul-Haq, who had helped the terrorists by providing them forged Indian passports and visa documents to enable them to proceed to West Asian countries. Noor-ul Haq was arrested by Hyderabad Police for sending India-based terrorists of Huji-B to join the ISIS. Hafiz Sheikh, another associate of Ali, was arrested by Kolkata Police for trafficking terrorists going to the Middle East. Police interrogation revealed that the Bangladeshi counterpart used to send photographs, names of the applicants, parentage, date of birth, etc., to Ali who forwarded these details to his two associates, Hafiz Sheikh and Iman Chowdhury, both residents of Kolkata. Both Sheikh and Chowdhury used to procure some Indian Passports and substitute the details of the passport holder with that of Bangladeshi nationals or Rohingya Muslims. After making the necessary changes they used to send the Indian passports through courier to the kingpin, Shaukat Ali. After collecting the forged passports Ali sent them to his associate Saddam Hussain to get Saudi Arabian visas stamped on them. Saddam then passed on the passports to Ibn-e Sultan who used to get multiple entry visas on the forged passports from the Saudi Arabian Embassy. They then sent these passports illegally to Bangladesh through their associate Amit Bodh Jha, a courier operating for radical Muslims. In this way, more than 20 persons per month were being sent to the Middle East. The syndicate used to transfer money through hawala operatives in Old Delhi and Suleman used to collect money from these hawala operatives on behalf of Shaukat Ali. The latter used to charge Rs. 1.5 lakhs to 2 lakhs for each passport. The money collected thus was shared with the other members of the recruiting syndicate, according to a source in Delhi police.

On 4th May, 2016, Delhi Police arrested three men suspected of having set up an Islamic State inspired jihadi group. They were allegedly plotting to attack the Hindon airbase of Indian Air Force. Allegedly, they also planned to carry out bomb strikes to avenge the 2013 riots in Muzaffarnagar (Uttar Pradesh). In this connection ten other suspects were detained for questioning. One of the suspects, Sajid Ahmad, resident of Bhajanpura was arrested after an explosion during the bomb-making process. One of his accomplices, Sameer Ahmed was arrested from the National Capital Region while another accomplice, Shakir Ansari, was arrested from Deoband. It may be mentioned that Deoband in Uttar Pradesh is the seat of the famous Islamic seminary. The three terrorists were reported to be in touch with Talha, son of Masood Azhar, in Pakistan through a WhatsApp group. Though the Intelligence Bureau had been monitoring the cell for over a year, the arrests took place only after Sajid suffered injuries from a bomb-making experiment which went wrong. An improvised explosive device was recovered from the men. The three jihadis had met in 2014 at a religious meeting organized by Abdul Sami Qasmi — a preacher who has been in prison since January, 2015.

Delhi has many mini-Molenbeeks (read no-go areas) where police are reluctant to enter because of the fear of resistance by anti-social elements, often patronized by political big wigs. Localities like Jamia Nagar, Batla House and the interior of Sarai Kale Khan are infamous 'no-go' areas in South Delhi where even pizza delivery boys are reluctant to go after sunset. On being questioned they reluctantly point to the instances where some aggressive rowdies grabbed the pizzas, but did not pay. There are numerous 'no-go' areas across the river in east Delhi, too. Needless to mention that the beat patrolling in these areas remains minimal due to reasons best left unstated, though shortage of manpower is one of the causes.

ISIS Threat on Eve of Republic Day, 2016

Ahead of the visit of the French President Francois Hollande on the occasion of India's Republic Day on 26th January, 2016, the threat of an attack by ISIS operators planted in India, loomed large over New Delhi. In a nationwide swoop, security agencies nabbed 12 terrorists suspected of having links with the ISIS. They were alleged to be involved in recruiting and financing Muslim youth for joining ISIS troops. The twelve suspects alleged to be associated with the ISIS included Mohammed Abdul Ahad, Mohammed Afzal and Suhail Ahmed from Bengaluru, Muhammed Shareef and Moinuddin Khan from Hyderabad, Muddabir Shaikh and Mohammed Hussain Khan from Mumbai, Mohammed Aleem form Lucknow (Uttar Pradesh), Imran from Aurangabad (Maharashtra), Asif Ali from Tamil Nadu,

Syed Mujahid and Najmal Huda from Karnataka.[10] Some electronic items including a laptop, hard discs, mobile phones and SIM cards, etc., were also seized from their family members which were sent for forensic examination. During investigations, the suspects disclosed certain useful clues about their connections abroad. The National Investigation Agency informed the court that the suspects had been regularly in touch with active members of the ISIS in Syria through Internet chatting via 'Skype', including the use of 'Signal' and 'Trillion' technologies. Ahead of the one-day visit of the French President Francois Hollande to Gurgaon a suspected Al-Qaeda mole was nabbed by Delhi Police from Haryana's Nuh district (formerly called 'Mewat'). Haryana Police have to maintain a special watch on the Muslim-dominated district because, during the last three years, a number of suspected jihadists had been arrested from there.

Dope Sold By Secularists

Lullabies are sung day and night by many political leaders and pro-Pakistani analysts from their multiple bandstands dismissing the jihadi threat as imaginary creation of a small lunatic fringe – a matter certainly not worth much thought. Pontificating that not many Indian Muslims could be sympathetic to the jihadi cause, they advise us to sit back and sing: "God is in His Heaven, all is right with the world". Their message seems to be: enjoy your morning breakfast of omelette and coffee, watch cricket on television during the day and applaud the histrionics of Bollywood sirens after dusk.

But can we continue to live in the dream world of cricket and Bollywood after experiencing the ongoing killings by rampaging jihadi hordes across India and the repeated targeting of Indian consulates in Afghanistan? Time has come for Hindus to open their eyes and face the grim reality writ large across the Indian horizon. Barely seven decades after independence, once again India's civilizational identity is precariously poised at the crossroads of history. The double whammy of rapid demographic changes and relentless jihadi attacks across the country, almost at will, have the potential to destroy the Hindu identity of India and tear asunder unity of the nation. Till a few years ago the depredations of jihadis were restricted largely to Kashmir valley and some parts of north-eastern India. But not any longer. During the UPA's ten years long rule the jihadi virus has spread all over India. Despite upgradation of the security systems after a change in the ruling political disposition at the Centre, even now no citizen feels safe and no temple is safe. On the day of every Hindu festival, retinues of men in khaki have to be present everywhere – even within temples. In sharp contrast, the threat of violent attack is far lower on the occasion of Muslim festivals.

A document procured by the American Media Institute from tribal areas of Pakistan warns that preparations for an attack on India are already under way. It further predicts that the attack will provoke an apocalyptic confrontation with the USA. Al Baghdadi believes that when the US tries to attack the ISIS that will unite the Ummah resulting in the final battle between Islam and the Kufir. Even if it is assumed that the ISIS might be bragging about the threat to start the process of ending the world by attacking India, Hindus must wake up to the growing threat which is real and imminent. Time has come to make all threatened 'kaffir' nations, including India and other world powers, to work unitedly to meet the challenge posed by this mammoth monster breathing savagery, fire and brimstone. It will be naive to ignore the future consequences of the rise of another savage power-center across the Middle East and South Asia, especially for a country like India, deeply faultlined by religious divide and with a huge population of nearly eighteen crore Muslims.

More importantly, many radical Muslim leaders of India like the notorious Owaisi brothers of Majlis-e-Ittehad-ul Muslimeen of Hyderabad and Imam Barkati of Tipu Sultan mosque of Kolkata keep on reminding us that their forefathers had ruled over Hindus for one thousand years. Akbaruddin Owaisi claimed that they hope to rule over India once again. Needless to mention, India has a long untranslatable history of animosity and politico-religious wars between the peace-loving Hindus and aggressive Muslims.

An in-depth analysis of the history of Islamic conquests in medieval era reveals that the most important reason for the dramatic success of Muslim armies in medieval times was their extensive use of gross savagery to terrorize and subjugate their frightened victims. Not only in India, but all over the world, Muslim armies used gross savagery as the most effective 'force-multiplier'. India's blood-soaked history is a speaking witness to the fact that Muslim armies indulged in large scale killings of Hindu warriors as well as commoners, followed by abduction and rape of the captured women. This was done on a mass scale across the sub-continent from Khyber Pass to Kanyakumari. In Europe the Balkans, Spain and Italy had to bear the burden of savagery unleashed by Muslim invaders for several centuries.

The objective of practicing savagery is to instill terror into the hearts of kaffirs (read non-Muslims), as candidly advocated by the retired Pakistani Brigadier, S. K. Malik, in chapter seven of his strategic tome, *The Quranic Concept of War.*[11] The retired Pakistani Brigadier openly advocated extensive use of terror to win wars in the following words :

> "Terror struck into the hearts of enemies is not a means, it is the end in itself. Once a condition of terror into the opponent's heart is obtained, hardly anything is left to be achieved. It is the point where the means and the end meet and merge. Terror is not a means of imposing decision upon the enemy; it is the decision we wish to impose upon him."

Brigadier Malik advocated the use of extensive terror by causing psychological and physical dislocation of infidels, as prescribed in the Quran. In ultimate analysis the terror should be used to dislocate and destroy the kaffir's faith.[12] This tactical advice for subjugating the enemies reveals the importance which Muslim rulers used to attach to destroying the temples and pilgrimage centers of Hindus. Recourse to unremitting savagery was also taken for destroying churches of the Christians in Egypt, Spain and across the Balkans. Presently it is being practiced by the ISIS in West Asia.

Foreign Fighters Joining ISIS

Till recently it was believed that roughly ten thousand Muslims from foreign countries joined the Islamic State. Many researchers, however, felt that the number could be far higher. The latest estimate compiled by the Soufan Group says that as many as 31,000 Muslims from at least 86 countries have travelled to Syria and Iraq since 2011 to fight for the Islamic State.[13]

Meanwhile Islamic State documents uncovered by the Sky News Television channel revealed valuable information about 23 different categories of ISIS fighters.[14] The 22,000 documents provide information about the countries travelled through by the ISIS warriors, their previous fighting experience, their special skills and who recommended them. The documents will lead security officials to those who radicalized the jihadis and facilitated their departure from parent countries. Entries in the documents on the forms include point of entry and who recommended recruits. Speaking about the discovery of the files, former Global Terrorism Operations Director at MI6, Richard Barrett, told Sky News that it was a fantastic coup – an absolute goldmine of information of enormous significance and interest to many people, particularly security and intelligence services. According to Richard Barrett there hasn't been anything like this since the discovery of the Mount Sinjar records in 2007 which covered about 700 ISIS fighters entering Iraq, all of whom were from Arab countries."

Afzal Ashraf, a counter-terrorism expert at the Royal United Services Institute, told the Sky News that the documents will give them an indication of not just who the recruits are and where they come from, but will be able to lead them to the individuals who radicalized them and facilitated their departure. "And it's those people that are really the key. It's these people that are capable of radicalizing and sending out foreign fighters in dozens, he said."[15]

Chapter 5

Dicey Role of Indian Fifth Columnists

"Oh Hindustan – We are 25 crores, you are 100 crores. Remove the police force for 15 minutes and we will show you who has more courage and strength. (Crowd rises up in standing ovation)! – Today, I have this mike in front of me. If tomorrow I hold something else, then there will be so much of bloodshed in this country which this country has not seen in the last 1000 years".

– Akbaruddin Owaisi at Nirmal (Telangana) on Dec. 22, 2012.

For several decades India has been *choc a bloc* with battalions of secessionists, fifth columnists and fellow travelers. Even after Partition many fifth columnists and fellow travelers remained entrenched in India and continued to strut across the political universe of our country. Unfortunately their hold on national politics grew manifold during the ten year long rule of Dr. Manmohan Singh and Sonia Gandhi. The establishment and rapid growth of Islamic State in West Asia has given a big boost to the morale of traitors and fellow-travelers operating in various parts of India. The number of young professionals pledging allegiance to ISIS and jihadi outfits has been rising sharply in many countries, including India. The Islamic State has successfully enticed a number of young Muslim professionals. Those who travelled to West Asia have reportedly been deputed for managing the group's refineries, banking system, communications and infrastructure requirements.

In her incisively researched Issue Brief Ms. Taruni Kumar of the Observer Research Foundation has analyzed the threat posed by ISIS. The analyst supplies ample evidence to prove that radicalization is not restricted to unschooled and economically deprived Muslims. In fact, most of the activists of the militant Islamic outfits, especially those belonging to the SIMI, the Indian Mujahideen and ISIS are highly educated professionals.[1] Ayman al-Zawahiri, the Al-Qaeda chief and one of the masterminds of the 9/11 terror attacks on USA is a trained surgeon. He is the best example of how a highly educated person, who could presumably lead a successful professional career, chose the path of Islamic terror.

According to Taruni Kumar nearly 35 percent of Al-Qaeda members were college educated and another 45 percent were engaged in skilled jobs. The Lashkar-e-Tayyeba, a global terrorist group based in Pakistan, has many professionals on its rolls who are qualified engineers, doctors and technicians. Most of them are either alumni of colleges and institutes run by the group or employed in the hospitals and engineering colleges operated by their affiliates. In India, the Indian Mujahideen (IM) had drawn most of its recruits from urban and educated backgrounds. So did the Students Islamic Movement of India (SIMI), another organization linked to terrorist activities in the country.

In late 2014 reports about a group of Indians, especially young professionals, joining ISIS started raising concerns in India's strategic circles. The increasing presence of Indians among the ISIS cadres and their associates was considered a significant departure from the past. Some analysts feel that in India, the jihadi movement is not an outcome of a particular interpretation of the Islamic texts and does not concern itself entirely with religion. They argue that it is the outcome of dissatisfaction among Muslims over political and social issues.

Prima facie, this line of thinking is seriously flawed because India has a long history of hostility and violent clashes between Hindus and Muslims. It is not a new phenomenon. Though many Muslim leaders keep blaming the Hindus for the backwardness of Muslims, the truth is that in four out of five major human development indices Muslims are better placed than Hindus. As already explained, the average Muslim lives 3 years longer than his Hindu counterpart and the incidence of infant and child mortality among Muslims is lower than among Hindus. It shows that Indian Muslims are better fed and economically better placed than their Hindu counterparts.

In her Issue Brief Taruni Kumar posed the following three questions for starting a purposeful debate about dimensions of the threat posed by the Islamic State to India[2] :

i)   Is there a marked trend among young Indian Muslim professionals to be drawn towards terrorism?

ii)   Is there a noticeable tendency among Indian Muslims towards joining the global jihadi causes?

iii) What will be the nature and extent of threats posed by these tendencies to India?

The commonsense response to the three strategic questions raised by Taruni Kumar is "yes", with a capital 'Y'. Unfortunately most Indian analysts tend to forget that a large majority of Indian Muslims had been radicalized even before India's partition in 1947. If Indian Muslims were not radicalized as early as 1920-21 there could have been no massacre of Hindus of Malabar by Moplahs, nor any Khilafat movement. Again if the Indian Muslims were indeed peace-loving and non-radicalized patriots, the Indian nation would not have been partitioned in 1947 amidst a gory bloodbath. The anti-national rantings of Akbaruddin Owaisi in December, 2012, at Nirmal in the Adilabad district of Andhra Pradesh were a clear indication of his morbid hatred for Hindus, depicting his total radicalization. And more importantly, the fact that his rabid vilification of Hindus was lustily cheered by a crowd of nearly 25-30 thousand Muslims irrefutably proved that India has an uncountable multitude of traitors, fifth columnists and fellow travelers. Again the cacophony created by several Urdu newspapers, grotesquely supported by a section of secularism-struck Hindu activists, against the death sentence awarded to Yakub Memon in July, 2015, further showed the strangle-hold of fifth columnists on the cerebral space of many Indians, mostly Hindus.

There have been a number of instance of the growing support for the Islamic State in the key state of Maharashtra. One such instance of the growing sympathy for ISIS came to public notice on 30 November, 2015, when protesting Muslim mobsters attacked the offices of the popular Marathi daily *Lokmat* in a number of cities across Maharashtra.[3] The newspaper is published from twelve cities of Maharashtra and claims to have the highest circulation. The reason was the publication of a cartoon lampooning the source of the funds raised by the Islamic State in the widely read newspaper Lokmat's supplement *Manthan*. To douse the fire of Muslim anger the editor of Lokmat immediately apologized to Muslims for the said cartoon. But the ruckus raised in support of ISIS did not die down. The offices of the leading Marathi newspaper group were attacked in many cities and copies of its Sunday edition were burnt in Mumbai, Dhule, Nandurbar, Malegaon and several other towns. Surprisingly the article titled *"ISIS cha Paisa"* meaning 'wherefrom comes ISIS money', infuriated the Muslim community of Maharashtra no end.[3] The extensive rioting that followed showed the goodwill and support which the Islamic State enjoys among Muslims of Maharashtra. An FIR was also registered against the newspaper editor and the cartoonist and extensive security was provided at all offices of the newspaper group by the police. Obviously these mobsters residing in several towns of Maharashtra are potential recruits for the Islamic State. An illustration of the cartoon published in Lokmat in November, 2015, is reproduced below.

The controversial illustration published in LOKMAT –
with grateful acknowledgments to Twitter

These developments and the information about the number of professionals and Indian Muslims joining the ISIS and allied militant groups indicate that within the next few years their number can become legion. Intelligence officials estimate that the India-based cell of ISIS, led by the one-time Indian Mujahideen operative Muhammad Shafi Armar (reportedly killed), was able to engage more than 700 persons in conversation on Internet and raised more than twenty identified volunteers for Islamic State.

What Attracts Muslims to ISIS

Every Muslim believes that he is a descendant of the world conquerors of yore and that his ancestors came from Arabia or Turkmenistan. He is constantly reminded of this by the Imams haranguing in mosques and madrasas that under Prophet Muhammad and following his demise, the foot soldiers of Islam had galloped across the globe like a desert maelstrom to conquer the Persian Sassanid Empire and subjugate Africa and parts of Europe. The average Muslim takes pride in the fact that his forebears defeated the crusaders, destroyed the Zoroastrian empire, enslaved the Hindus of Indian subcontinent, and annexed Malaysia and Indonesia. To add fuel to the jihadi fire, there is an intense yearning deep down in the hearts of most Muslims to recapture their lost glory and establish supremacy of Islam. They don't want to live in a democratic set up under the norms designed by the western civilization and kaffir faiths.

Another reason which attracts Muslim youth to ISIS is that Islam is essentially a 'clash and conquest' oriented religion. Ever since its advent in seventh century, jihad or holy war against kaffirs has been its *leit motif*. Within one hundred years of Prophet Muhammad's death Islamic armies conquered the eastern and southern shores of Mediterranean and annexed the Iberian Peninsula and Spain. They destroyed the Zoroastrian Empire, attacked the Indian sub-continent and overran Sindh. A long spell of nearly one thousand years, from seventh to seventeenth century, was an era of the glory and grandeur of Islam. To the chagrin of the Islamic world, between eighteenth and twentieth centuries the Christian nations of Europe turned the tables on Islam by capturing a number of Muslim countries. Finally after the abolition of the Caliphate by Kemal Ataturk in 1924 the glory of Islam went into sunset mode. That setback continues to rankle in the minds of the Muslims worldwide. An urge to restore the long lost glory of Islam continues to fire the imagination of Muslim youth. That yearning prompts the hordes of Muslim youth to wage jihad against non-Muslims by joining the Islamic State.

Enticing Educated Youth

In her Issue Brief Taruni Kumar has pointed out that the educated Muslim terrorists pose greater threat to India than those who have a limited educational and lesser technical skills. A militant organization that has cadres from the fields of engineering, medicine and computer science will be a far more difficult entity to deal with. Sound knowledge of engineering can help terrorist groups build more sophisticated weapons and systems and can cause more havoc across the country than the less skilled Muslims. The know-how in technological fields like mechanical engineering, electronics and chemicals can prove invaluable to such Islamic organizations. In addition, the availability of medical aid from within the group reduces the chances of defection of fighters in need of medical attention. Proficiency in computer technology and the digital world is one of the biggest assets that a terror group can possess today.

In the year 2014 there were multiple media reports claiming that several youth were being recruited by the ISIS from Kerala, Tamil Nadu, Maharashtra and Karnataka. Some of them were being trained allegedly in Pakistan, Iraq and Syria to fight as 'fedayeen' of the Islamic State. Subsequently a National Investigating Agency report estimated that nearly 300 Indian youth had been enlisted by the ISIS. The real number, however, is now believed to be much larger. As stated by the strategic analyst Madhav Nalapat, in an article published on January 24, 2015, in *The Sunday Indian*, New Delhi, by then nearly one thousand Indian Muslims had joined the jihadi troops of al-Baghdadi. Official sources, however, have not, so far confirmed the actual figure. The ISIS recruiters have been working overtime in Uttar Pradesh, Assam, West Bengal, Kerala, Seemandhra. Telangana and Maharashtra. Meanwhile, Dabiq, the official journal of the ISIS has claimed that nearly two lakh seventy thousand Indian Muslims are regular viewers of their websites and were reading the messages of the group posted on Internet. That huge figure shows the mindboggling reach of ISIS among Indian Muslims. That very year, in the month of June an Al Qaeda ideologue, Asim Umar, had issued a video in Urdu which exhorted Muslims of Jammu and Kashmir and other Indian States to join the jihad being waged against India. One video with Hindi, Tamil and Urdu subtitles, posted on jihadi forums and YouTube, featured a Canadian jihadi named Abu Muslim. Another video seeking Indian volunteers with Hindi subtitles featured the ISIS spokesman Shaikh Adnani.

Taruni Kumar has emphasized the following five aspects of the call of the Islamic State to the Muslims of the world, including Indians, and the resultant threat to the Indian nation.

(i) Two common arguments advanced to explain radicalization of Muslim youth are economic deprivation and lack of education. Several recent studies presented by Taruni Kumar, however, comprehensively rebut the above mentioned facile arguments by offering evidence to the contrary.

(ii) In February, 2004 the Pew Research Center's Global Attitudes Project conducted public opinion surveys on about 1,000 respondents each, in Jordan, Morocco, Pakistan and Turkey. One of the questions concerned suicide bombings carried out against Americans and other westerners in Iraq and whether or not these were 'justifiable'. The results of the survey showed that people with a higher level of education were more likely to justify suicide attacks against the westerners.

(iii) An argument can be advanced that those who decide to join terrorist organizations may be influenced by a set of complex factors including economic frustration, religious beliefs, or a desire for a revolutionary change from secularism to an Islamized polity. But can it be used for propagating violence?

(iv) Membership of an organization which pursues these goals through extremist means and violence is a commitment that goes beyond a person's chosen profession or educational background. This is evident in the fact that such membership requires absolute loyalty to a cause that may be external to one's own personal context within which a person's professional and educational background are located. This, too, is a thoroughly unconvincing argument.

(v) One of the major requirements for terrorists to survive in today's globalized and technology-intensive world is that the jihadis ought to be educated. They should also possess enough technical competence to be able to circumvent governmental controls and high-tech surveillance systems.

In early 1980s Saade-din Ibrahim, a well-known human rights activists of Egypt, had interviewed 34 members of two violent groups in Egypt: the Military Academy group and the Al-Takfir group, whose members were imprisoned in the late 1970s. Of these, 29 volunteers were either graduates or university students. Among them were nine engineers, six doctors, five agronomists, two pharmacists; two studying technical military science and one studying literature.

Nearly all Muslim terror cells in India have been drawing their cadres from the Students Islamic Movement of India (SIMI). The SIMI emerged as the student wing of the Jamaat-e-Islami-e-Hind

(JIH) in April 1977. From the beginning of its campaign, SIMI has been stating that the organization's preaching and practice of Islam was 'a political project'. The organization was sure that in the long term, the Caliphate would have to be re-established as without it the practice of Islam would remain incomplete. SIMI's propaganda found appeal amongst a growing number of lower-middle and middle-class urban young men.

An organization that has recruited many of its members from SIMI is the Indian Mujahideen. These die-hard jihadis are connected through ideological similarities and personal links and are mostly under the age of 40. They are often trained in Pakistan by the Lashkar-e-Tayeba and many of them have been highly educated professionals before being recruited. Many high-profile members of the Indian Mujahideen and SIMI are computer-literate and possess impressive backgrounds, holding lucrative private-sector jobs. Mumbai-based Abdul Subhan Qureshi, aka, Tauqeer, an Indian Mujahideen leader, is an example of those who do not fit in the stereotype of a madrasa-educated extremist. He graduated from Antonio De Souza High School in 1988. He also has a Diploma in Industrial Electronics and has earned a specialized software maintenance qualification. At the independent computer firm where he worked, co-workers said, Qureshi was 'exceptional'. Three years into his professional life, Qureshi managed to quadruple his pay and handled quite a few major independent projects like an intranet implementation for Bharat Petro-Chemicals carried out by Wipro in 1999. This background seems out of place, considering that Qureshi was among the primary suspects for masterminding the Bengaluru, Ahmedabad and Delhi blasts of 2008.

The Indian Mujahideen has several key figures having similar backgrounds. For instance, Riyaz Shahbandri aka Riyaz Bhatkal, a co-founder of the group, holds a degree in engineering from the Sabu Siddique College in Mumbai. Yasin Bhatkal, who co-founded the Indian Mujahideen and was involved in terror attacks in Ahmedabad,

Surat, Bengaluru, Pune, Delhi and Hyderabad, was an engineering graduate from Karnataka. Atif Amin, an Indian Mujahideen commander killed in the September, 2008, shootout in Batla House encounter with the Delhi Police, was from a middle-class background with an English-medium education and a college degree. Similarly Qayamuddin Kapadia, who was tried for his alleged role in organizing the Indian Mujahideen attacks in Gujarat, is a graphics designer. Mohammad Abrar Qasim was a dentist before he joined SIMI in 1993.

To set up a cell of the Indian Mujahideen in Bengaluru, six qualified IT workers were recruited through a front organization called 'Sarani'. Mansoor Peerbhoy, who had produced and electronically sent the manifestos of Indian Mujahideen after the 2005 serial blasts in Delhi and elsewhere comes from an educated well-to-do family. He was a computer engineer working at Yahoo's Indian office. According to investigators, Peerbhoy, 31, was the head of a 'media terror cell' comprising "highly qualified, computer savvy people belonging to good and educated families". One of his brothers is a doctor in the UK and the other is an architect. In March, 2014, two engineering college students from Jaipur were arrested with a huge cache of explosives who were affiliated with the Indian Mujahideen.

ISIS Strikes Roots in India

Events of the years 2014 and 2015 point to significant changes in the process of recruitment to terrorist groups from India. In this connection two developments are noteworthy.

One major development is that some Indian Muslims are already beginning to join global terrorist groups like Islamic State (ISIS). For the present their number may be small, but the latest trends show a growing inclination among many Indian Muslims to participate in the global jihadi campaigns. Earlier, the distance between the Indian Muslim population and the global jihadi groups was evident in the small number of SIMI cadres joining the Al-Qaeda despite the latter's consistent attempts at recruitment from India. The Indian Mujahideen, though backed by Pakistan, highlighted mostly the domestic grievances of Indian Muslims. The global ambitions of the ISIS, however, have acquired far greater appeal for the Muslim youth of India.

The second notable change which should worry the government is the manner in which Internet is being used by the swarms of terrorists enlisted, trained and nurtured by the cyber experts working for Al-Baghdadi. When the Indian Mujahideen used Internet as a tool, it could do nothing more than send messages to the media, communicate amongst members and put out propaganda handouts. In those days, Internet was not the only mode used for communication and indoctrination. Personal meetings and consultations, too, were useful tools for them.

But in the case of the young men joining the ISIS, all indoctrination and planning is conducted online. Internet has become today's principal tool of recruitment and indoctrination for global jihad launched by the ISIS. Among the four men arrested in November, 2014, by the Maharashtra police for joining the ISIS, barring one, who was a school dropout, the rest happened to be well-schooled. Arif Majeed, a 23-year old Muslim from Navi Mumbai, Maharashtra who fought in Iraq and Syria for the Islamic State in 2014, was a civil engineering student. His father is a doctor with a clinic in Mumbai. His elder sister is also a doctor at a well-known hospital in the city.

Three other young men had left the country with him to fight for ISIS. Fahad Shaikh was a mechanical engineering graduate whose father was a doctor. Aman Tandel was an engineering student and his father was an engineer with the Indian Railways. Another ISIS operator, Mehdi Mansoor Biswas, arrested from Bengaluru for running a pro-Islamic State Twitter account in December, 2014, was a 24-year old computer engineer. Mehdi Biswas, however, did not seem to have any direct links to the militant group, although his Twitter handle, '@Shami Witness' was the extremist group's most influential publicity tool having some 17,700 followers.

A number of the accused Mujahids mentioned in the said report were radicalized through Internet, or at religious meetings, or through the influence of families and friends. Ever since the rise of ISIS many Indian youth have also been influenced by the idea of global jihad against infidels (read kaffirs).

Ace Fifth Columnist Zakir Naik

A suspected fifth columnist operating with impunity in India is Dr. Zakir Naik, founding President of the Islamic Research Foundation, who runs an anti-India campaign through his tele-channel, Peace TV, from Dubai. The fire-brand radical preacher has been called the rock star of Islamic tele-evangelism. He has a huge following among Indian Muslims. It is said that he has a following of nearly 10 to 15 million Indian Muslims. In any case, Zakir Naik has 15 million followers on his Facebook and Twitter accounts which shows his popularity. When the news broke out that Maharashtra Government might take legal action against the notorious tele-evangelists, demonstrations were organized in Patna, Ranchi and Chennai in his support. In Patna many Muslim activists courted arrest after creating a ruckus on the roads. The fundamentalist outfit, Popular Front of India, also joined the protests.

It may be recalled that the Hyderabad-born lady recruiter Afshan Jabeen, working for ISIS, repatriated from the United Arab Emirates (UAE) and arrested in September, 2015, was also influenced by the preaching of Zakir Naik. The commitment of the notorious tele-evangelist to the destabilization of Indian nation is reflected in his pronouncements reproduced below.

- Islam is the supreme religion to which all Indians must subscribe.
- All other religions are inferior to Islam and therefore fit to be condemned.
- India should be ruled in accordance with Sharia law.
- Speaking about Osama bin Laden, he stated in a YouTube video that if "Bin Laden is fighting the enemies of Islam, I am for him." Every Muslim should be a terrorist, emphasized Dr. Zakir Naik.
- Muslims can have sex with captured kaffir female slaves because it is halal in Islam.
- While Naik appreciates that people of other religions do allow Muslims to freely practice Islam in their countries, he forbids the propagation of other religions within an Islamic state because all other faiths are false.
- Regarding building of churches or temples in Muslim countries, Naik argues that how can the building of churches and temples be allowed when their religion is false?
- Those who leave Islam and who propagate a non-Islamic faith and speak against Islam should be put to death.
- A husband has the right to beat his wife as ordained in the Quran but the beating should not be too harsh.

The wonky utterances of Zakir Naik reveal his dangerous anti-national mindset. Yet, so powerful indeed is the hold of jihadi ideology on the Muslim community of India that this merchant of hate has lakhs of followers. On top of it there are many anti-Hindu Hindus like the Congress politician Digvijay Singh and the Bollywood icon Mahesh Bhat who are admirers of Dr. Zakir Naik.

Although Peace TV was banned in the year 2012, no restrictions were placed on his inflammatory speeches. In sharp contrast with the latitude given to him in India Zakir Naik was denied entry into the United Kingdom and Canada in June, 2010, because of his rabid outpourings against various religions. While banning his entry into United Kingdom, the then Home Secretary Theresa May had cited his "unacceptable behaviour" as the reason for ban on his entry. Incidentally Theresa May is now the Prime Minister of the United Kingdom.

In the year 2008, Satyapal Singh, the former Police Commissioner of Mumbai, who is now a Member of Parliament, had sent a detailed note highlighting the anti-national activities of Zakir Nair to Ministry of Home Affairs. He claims to have also referred to violation of the Foreign Contributions (Regulation) Act by the Islamic Research Foundation headed by Dr. Naik. But his report was ignored by the central government led by Dr. Manmohan Singh. *Prima facie* the open support of the heavy weight Congress leader Digvijay Singh and some other politicians to Zakir Naik facilitated the pushing of the said report under the carpet.

Recently the broadcasting of Peace TV Bangla and entry of the notorious tele-evangelist has been banned in Bangladesh, too. It is alleged that the terrorists who attacked the upmarket Café in Dhaka on July 1, 2016, and killed 20 persons had been indoctrinated by the preachings of Zakir Naik. One of the attackers involved in the Café killings in Dhaka's high-security Gulshan area was Rohan Imtiaz. He had quoted Naik in a Facebook post in January, 2016, in which all Muslims were urged to become terrorists.

The Home Minister of Bangladesh, Asaduzzaman Khan, said that the government had asked intelligence agencies to investigate Zakir Naik's possible role in the Dhaka attack. He added that investigators were also probing Naik's financial transactions and the funding of his group in Bangladesh.

At long last the activities of Naik's Mumbai-based Islamic Research Foundation have come under the scanner of the Maharashtra police and the Indian Home Ministry. There are allegations that the huge funds received by the Islamic Research Foundation from abroad are being spent on political activities and radicalizing the Muslim youth. At one stage Zakir Naik had indicated that he would return to India from Saudi Arabia to respond to the charges of disturbing peace and anti-national activities. But ultimately, he decided not to return to India because he feared arrest and prosecution.

Kashmir and Burhan Wani's Death

The Kashmir Valley continues to be a major zone of religion-based fault-line conflicts in India. There have been frequent displays of ISIS flags and jihadi symbols along with pro-Pakistani activity by militant groups in the Kashmir Valley, especially in Srinagar and many other towns, after Friday prayers. The State has a wide array of fifth columnists and fellow travellers, too.

Burhan Wani was, by far one of the most wanted jihadis operating in the Kashmir Valley. He acquired a larger than life image by gathering a group of nearly fifty Muslim youth, many of whom were proficient in using social media and weapon-use, for propagating a new wave of militancy. Along with his band of hand picked terrorists Burhan used to post on the internet, pictures of themselves in combat fatigues, armed with automatic weapons, thereby promoting defiance of law among youngsters. On one occasion he was seen holding the black flag of ISIS, though his allegiance to the dreaded outfit was never established. But he did manage to start a new trend of villagers coming out in support of terrorists locked in gun battles with security forces which made the latter's task more difficult.

On 8 July, 2016, there was a fierce encounter in the wilds of Kokarnag between a detachment of 19 Rashtriya Rifles (Sikh Light Infantry) and the notorious terrorist hiding in a house. The encounter lasted for nearly 2 hours and around 7.30 p.m. Burhan was killed. Along with two other armed militants he had been hiding in a house which was surrounded by the army. When he came out in a bid to escape, he was gunned down.

By allowing a public burial of Burhan Wani, a monumental tactical mistake was committed by the State Government. The funeral of the slain jihadist was attended by nearly thirty thousand mourners who set the valley literally on fire after returning from Burhan's Namaz-e-Janaza. After his burial, a wave of gross violence and stone pelting at the police and the army, broke out in Kashmir valley in which 80 civilians and one policeman was killed. There were well-planned attacks on several police stations and security posts, including army bunkers. The families of policemen are being openly threatened and their houses targeted. According to unconfirmed reports nearly 70 rifles and A-47s were looted by the jihadists. The number of injured was more than ten thousand people. Among them nearly six thousand were civilians who received injuries caused by the pellet guns used by the security forces. Unfortunately many civilians received eye injuries, too. At the same time, more than 4,000 security personnel were injured due to stone pelting by violent mobs. For nearly two weeks there was a forced lock down in the Valley due to the call for 'bandh' given by the leaders of the Hurriyat and other secessionist outfits.

Targeting policemen and security forces by relentless stone pelting has been the favourite weapon of jihadi mobsters. The strategy used by the militants is to keep stone-pelting tender-aged children in front of mobs. There are rumours that young children are being trained in madrasas and mosques to target the security forces and provoke them by hurling filthy abuses at them – even try to urinate at the members of police forces in order to provoke them to use force. The whole drill of harassing and provoking the police personnel is a well organized jihadi campaign.

Kashmir has a long history of militancy and violence. A Pakistan propelled jihad raged in the Valley in 1989 and 1990 which led to the ethnic cleansing of Hindus. More than four lakh Kashmiri Pandits were forced to migrate out of their ancient homeland and to date they have not been able to go back despite phoney assurances given by the State government as well as the central government.

Many myopic and inadequately read politicians and the media commentators keep blaming the unrest in Kashmir on lack of employment opportunities and poor economic development, etc. They keep advocating grant of more autonomy and endless negotiations while separatists run riot.

The biggest surprise was the singing the bogus song of more autonomy by P. Chidambram, the former Home Minister of India, who ought to have known better. But Chidambram is not the only political heavy-weight recommending molly coddling of violent jihadis. He is in the good company of several top leaders belonging to Janata Dal United, CPI (M), Samajwadi Party, Muslim League, the Nationalist Congress Party (NCP), et al. And to the chagrin of the beleaguered and battle-scarred security forces there are battalions of journalists pleading for appeasing the weapon-wielding killers like Burhan Wani. No wonder, our vision-bereft forefathers remained slaves of invaders for more than one thousand years.

They too must have been afflicted by the virus called political correctness aka self-deception !

It is not known how many of the Wahabi preachers out of the 25,000 Maulanas who visited India in 2013 (mostly from West Asian countries) had travelled to Kashmir valley to preach to the youth studying in madrasas. According to a reliable source, some of them did manage to go to Kashmir. It needs to be ascertained whether they did preach Wahabi Islam in a bid to radicalize the youth studying in madrasas. Their role needs to be scrutinized and lessons learnt – at least for the future.

The political busy bodies and most journalists have failed to realize that the Islamic doctrine of jihad is the root cause of repetitive violence which sears the overwhelmingly Muslim-populated valley. What India is facing in Kashmir is not a campaign for 'azadi'. Nor can it be categorized as a clamour for more autonomy. It is the monster called jihad – launched for total Islamization of Kashmir. Unfortunately even after the violent ethnic cleansing of Hindus in 1990 by armed mobsters the Indian strategist could not diagnose the Kashmir problem. As long as the global jihad remains in fast forward mode, Kashmir valley will continue to erupt in violence and mayhem. The malaise called global jihad and violence in Kashmir are intertwined.

The old Defence Ministry files reveal that between 1996 and 2001, nearly 626 foreign militants were killed in Kashmir while battling the Indian security forces.[4] Some of them came from distant lands like Sudan, Libya and Egypt. The overwhelming majority, however, came from Pakistan and Afghanistan.[5] The appeaser politicians should explain why would militants from distant countries like Sudan and Libya come to India for seeking redressal of the grievances of Kashmiris? Our self-styled intellectuals refuse to understand the implications of jihad even after seeing how on 1st July, 2016, innocent kaffirs were butchered in Dhaka because they could not recite 'Kalima' and verses from the Quran. All those who plead for granting more autonomy to the State are barking up the wrong tree. Financially every Kashmiri Muslim is better off than his counterpart in other States of India. He is better placed than the Hindus and Buddhists of Jammu and Ladakh regions, too. Then what is the all fuss about, why does Kashmir Valley burn? It is time that the Indian government and our inadequately-read secularized politicians and analysts understood what lies at the root of the Kashmir problem. Showering dollops of more autonomy and candy loads of financial grants cannot appease the die-hard militants waging anti-India war in

Kashmir. Can the fire of jihad be extinguished by appeasement ? No, never, ever. With the fast-paced globalization of jihad, it is no longer possible to win the support of the jihad obsessed Muslims of Kashmir.

Lady Recruiter for ISIS

Last year a 37 year old lady recruiter of the ISIS, Afshan Jabeen, was arrested by police at Hyderabad airport on September 11, 2015, after she was deported from Dubai along with her husband and three children. She had been a resident of Toli Chowk area of the city and was remanded to 14 days judicial custody. The police are trying to locate her associates to gather information about Muslim youth, along with another accused Salman Mohiuddin. Both of them were in touch with some ISIS aspirants through social media and were motivating them to join the ISIS. Afshan was using a fictitious Christian name, Nicky Joseph, and claimed to be a British national. During police interrogation she admitted that she was running Facebook groups to lure Muslim youth into joining the ISIS. She candidly confessed to being a strong supporter of the Islamic State because the group was stopping the Syrian President Assad from committing atrocities on Sunnis. Like many devout Muslims she was keen to ensure the establishment of Sharia across India. Police came to know about her activities in January, 2015, when an America-returned engineer, Salman, was arrested at Hyderabad airport while trying to fly to Dubai. The Muslim zealot further disclosed that along with a woman he was planning to go to Syria to join ISIS. After the arrest of her accomplice Salman, intelligence officers maintained a close watch on the online activities of Nicky Joseph. After discovering her real identity – that she was not Nicky Joseph, but Afshan Jabeen, the Intelligence Bureau tipped the security authorities of United Arab Emirates about her identity and pro-ISIS activities. The UAE authorities decided to deport her to India, after interrogating her.

Sustained interrogation revealed that Afshan had been in touch with at least nine activists of the Islamic State located in Mumbai, Hyderabad, Delhi, Bengaluru and Kashmir who have been active on Facebook.[5] She admitted that she used to follow the speeches and writings of the chief of Jaish-e-Muhammad, Maulana Masood Azhar, the Indian tele-evangelist of Islam Dr. Zakir Naik, Mohammed Mizanur Rahman of the United Kingdom, writer Yasir Qadhi of Pakistani origin, the controversial preacher Anjem Choudhary of the United Kingdom and a fundamentalist South African writer, Ahmed Deedat. Afshan further claimed that she came into contact with Salman Mohiuddin after posting a comment on a video speech of Dr. Zakir Naik on YouTube. According to Cyberabad police, Afshan is a co-accused in the case involving Salman Mohiuddin, also from Hyderabad, who was arrested in January 2015, while trying to board a flight to Dubai to go to Syria. Both of them had allegedly indoctrinated several Indian youth through social media.

Tamil Nadu in Grip of Jihad

Fifth columnists and fellow-travelers have struck deep roots in several parts of India. That the virus has travelled in a big way across South India is evident from the notoriety earned by the coastal town of Bhatkal in Karnataka for spreading terror across the country. A radical outfit called Tamil Nadu Thowheed Jamath, having lakhs of members, gave a call on 28th July, 2015, for launching a 'Battle of Badr' in India. It is led by Jainulabdeen, a fundamentalist to the core, who preaches violence to promote the cause of Islam. It may be recalled that in the past the Egypt-Israel War and the Taliban offensives in Afghanistan were all termed as "Battles of Badr" by radical Muslims. Even the police are extra cautious in dealing with them. Many among them are potential volunteers for ISIS.[6]

Quran as Key to Sharia Rule

By and large a high percentage of Indian Muslims are excessively charmed by the sharia law. Their yearning for the Quran-based laws is no way lesser than their co-religionists living across the border in Pakistan. A recent survey by the Pew Research Center, New York, revealed that in Muslim countries an overwhelming percentage of citizens are in favour of Sharia law based on the guidelines prescribed in the Quran. An analysis of the acceptance of Quranic laws over the secular laws in ten countries having significant Muslim populations revealed some interesting trends. In many Islam-dominated countries an overwhelming percentage of Muslims showed a marked preference for a system based on the guidelines provided in the Quran. For instance, in Pakistan nearly 78 percent people were found to be in favour of the Quranic laws. In the Palestinian territory the percentage was 65%, in Jordan it was 54% , while in Malaysia it was 52%.

In Pakistan, the Palestinian territories, Jordan, Malaysia and Senegal, roughly half or more of the full population say that laws in their country should strictly follow the teachings of the Quran. No such survey has been conducted in India. But many analysts feel that if such a survey was held in India the percentage of those favouring Sharia law could be as high as among the Pakistani Muslims. The insistence of most Muslims on continuing the practice of triple talaq and denying the right of equality to Muslim women shows that their commitment to Sharia law is no less than that of their co-religionists in Pakistan.

The fact that nearly half or more population in the ten countries surveyed said that the laws in their countries should strictly follow the teachings of the Quran demonstrates the deep imprint of the Quran on the Muslim masses. This opinion is significantly high in the Islamic Republic of Pakistan (78%) which is closely followed by the Palestinian territories (65%). The monumental support for the Islamic

State bodes ill for the world peace. It is bound to make life difficult for the kaffir communities.

What Makes India Prime Target ?

Hostility between Muslims and Hindus is a 1200 years old festering sore which led to the partition of the country in 1947. It was fondly hoped that the creation of a theocratic State will pacify the aggressive Muslims of India. But the hiatus between the two communities has refused to die down even after Partition because Pakistan has floated a number of militant outfits to subvert India. Though branded as 'non-state actors' the outfits like Lashkar-e-Tayyeba, Jaish-e-Muhammad, Indian Mujahideen, United Jihad Council, Dukhtran-e-Millat and many other groups have been nurtured by Pakistan. In fact, jihadi terrorism has been the major plank of Pakistan's state policy which aims at debilitating and destroying India. The targeting of Indian citizens by senseless bombings in a most audacious manner has been practiced by the Pakistani establishment during the last 70 years. The crescendo of violent attacks increased tremendously during the ten year rule of Dr. Manmohan Singh and Sonia Gandhi.

The Islamic State is not the first challenger to the Hindu identity of India. Islam has waged multiple wars against Hindus of Indian sub-continent ever since Muhammad bin Qasim attacked Sind and Multan in 712 A.D. Despite dozens of attempts made by the secularized Hindu leaders like Gandhiji and Pandit Nehru during the last century to mollycoddle the Muslim fundamentalists, the divide between the two communities has increased. How can one forget that in the Moplah rebellion of 1920s thousands of Hindus were murdered and their womenfolk outraged, as highlighted by Dr. Ambedkar in his book, 'Pakistan and Partition of India', while the Congress leaders slept? Finally the growing hostilities between the Hindus and Muslims led to the partition of the subcontinent into two countries, India and

Pakistan in 1947. But even after the creation of Pakistan as the holy land for Indian Muslims, the anti-Hindu depredations of multiple Islamic outfits floated and nurtured by Pakistan have continued unchecked and unabated. The avowed aim of Pakistan and multiple jihadi outfits floated by it is to destroy the Hindus whom they dub as 'kaffirs'. It is a pity, nay a shame, that even after the humiliating mauling of Mumbai by ten Pakistan-trained commandos on November 26, 2008, and two attacks on Pathankot in the year 2015, we Indians have not learnt any lesson.

The emergence of Islamic State has added a new dimension to the geopolitical map of Asia. The new Islamic entity is focussed on annexing the entire Middle East and northern Africa. After seizing Europe it promises to overrun India during the next five years. Al-Baghdadi has been administering the Caliphate quite satisfactorily, although its mode of governance is based on the 1400 years old Islamic laws. The data available in the public domain shows that more than 30,000 men and women have reportedly joined the ranks of ISIS. They have travelled to West Asia from more than 80 countries. Among the nations contributing jihadi warriors 11 happen to be non-Muslim countries. In true Islamic tradition all minorities have been declared as dhimmies. They are forced to pay the poll tax called jiziya and reduced to the status of second class citizens. The Yazidis, dubbed as devil worshippers, have become third class citizens. In fact, a paper produced by the leaders of the group in 2006 clearly stated that improving the quality of the people's religion was a more important task than improving the quality of their life.

Enumerated below are the major reasons which are likely to prompt Islamic State to attack India :

- India has a 200 million strong Muslim community which constitutes the third largest catchment area in the world for recruiting jihadi volunteers. The huge numbers make it a fertile hunting ground for recruits by groups like ISIS, Al Qaeda and Lashkar-e-Tayeba, et al.

- India has a large number of migrants working in the Gulf countries. Their number could be between 50 to 60 lakh or more. A vast majority of them are Muslims who could be a major source of recruitment for ISIS. Quite a few of them have joined ISIS. In addition, every year lakhs of Indian Muslims go to Saudi Arabia for Haj and many of them get radicalized after interacting with hard core Islamists coming from other countries for Haj.

- India has a long history of Islamic hostility towards the idol-worshipping Hindus. For 1200 years Hindus remained engaged in war against Muslim invaders and in the process suffered enormous persecution at the hands of the conquerors. In sharp contrast, the Zoroastrian empire of Persia was overrun and ravaged in less than two decades and most Parsis forcibly converted to Islam. In India, however, despite countless battles waged for centuries the invaders could not fully subdue the Hindus. The invaders could not seize the whole subcontinent, nor convert the entire population to the creed of their Prophet. The old wounds inflicted by the incessant killings and plunder by Muslim invaders continue to pain the Hindu psyche even today. In recent years the hostility between the two communities has increased enormously due to repetitive terrorist attacks and machinations of the Pakistan's spy agency, Inter-Services Intelligence (ISI). The unending jihad in Kashmir has further magnified the Hindu-Muslim divide.

- In recent years Internet has emerged as a powerful instrument for online training and motivation of the fanaticism inclined Muslims. India has a fast-growing number of Internet and smartphone users. It is the second largest smartphone market in the world and is expected to have a smart phone-user base totaling more than 650 million by 2019. This adds to the possibility of online radicalized

Indian Muslims joining ISIS. This phenomenon is already visible in Jammu & Kashmir, Maharashtra, Kerala, West Bengal, Tamil Nadu, et.al. Lately Indian geeks have become the third highest users of Internet in the world. Therefore numbers of radicalized Muslims are bound to grow because access to Internet is no longer restricted to the citizens belonging to higher socio-economic strata.

- Caliph Al-Baghdadi has been openly threatening to overrun India because of the alleged persecution of Muslims in India. A map has been circulated by ISIS which depicts India as a part of their associate mini-Caliphate called Wilayat Khorasan. The Islamic State is now working on the project Wilayat Hind which specifically aims at lighting the prairie fire of Jihad across India. Baghdadi's plan to attack India is now a project in works !

- India happens to be the only democratic nation in South Asia which stands as a powerful obstacle to the advancement of Caliphate's global jihad to conquer the world. By defeating the Indian State, ISIS will score its most spectacular victory worldwide and send a tough message to all 'kaffir' nations to submit to Islam. Subjugating India will considerably enhance Islamic State's stature and threaten the stability of the region, according to Bruce Riedel, a senior fellow with the Brookings Institution. Bruce Riedel who served in America's Central Investigation Agency for more than thirty years, feels that attacking India will be the Holy Grail for the soldiers of Islamic State. Therefore it is bound to happen, he argues.

- The recent trend in India's domestic politics where radical Islam is being openly propagated, even lionized, will invite ISIS to Indian shores. Pro-jihad utterings of fundamentalists like Akbaruddin Owaisi, his brother Assauddin Owaisi, Imam Barkati of Tipu Sultan Mosque in Kolkata and many others of their ilk are straws in the wind. The rising tide of Islamism bodes ill for India's future.

The politico-religious ruckus which erupted in the Jawaharlal Nehru University in February, 2016, and the communal clashes which pock-marked the academic atmosphere of the National Institute of Technology at Srinagar in April, 2016, point to the growing influence of radical elements in educational institutions. A disturbing aspect of the rising tide of anti-national activities in educational institutions is the support given to the radical groups by self-styled secularist column-writers and anchors of tele-media.

The die has been cast by Islamic State. Now it is for the Indian nation to pick up the gauntlet !

Use of Grievance Politics

The incessant fulminations by Majlis Ittehad-ul-Muslimeen (MIM), Popular Front of India and many similar outfits have added grist to the mill of pro-jihadi groups. At the same time, there has been a surge in the hostility against Hindus due to the frequently voiced allegations of intolerance played out by our partisan media. Many Muslim leaders have been fueling the false propaganda about marginalization of the Muslim community in India in a bid to instigate the Muslim youth to join the jihadi campaign. In fact, the false and fabricated report of Justice Sachar has been used extensively for radicalizing more and more Muslim youngsters and alienating them from the national mainstream. The fudged findings of Justice Sachar have totally convinced the Muslim masses that they are being discriminated against by the government at the behest of Hindus. To put it mildly, the contribution of Justice Sachar's findings in raising the level of hatred towards Hindus among Muslim masses has been immense – even mind-boggling. The truth, however, is that according to the data available in public domain, Muslims are better placed than Hindus in almost all major human development indices. They live longer and are better fed.

Last year on 31st August, 2015, Shri Hamid Ansari, Vice President of India, made some wild accusations about the so-called backwardness of Muslims while addressing a gathering of Muslim scholars in Delhi. The falsity of his accusations is evident from the fact that according to the latest data in public domain there has been a quantum jump in the life expectancy of average Muslim vis a vis his Hindu counterpart. Presently the life expectancy of an average Muslim is 68 years, while that of an average Hindu is barely 65 years. In 1998–99 on average a Muslim used to live only 1.2 years longer than an average Hindu, but now he lives three years longer than his Hindu counterpart. During the last 16 years the longevity of Muslims has stolen a huge march over the longevity of Hindus. Again the percentage of infant and child mortality among Muslims has always been lower than among Hindus confirming that Muslims are better fed. Yet most Muslim leaders keep trotting out the falsehood of economic backwardness by quoting Justice Sachar's convoluted findings. They keep on playing the political card of grievance politics.

Role of Al Isabah

The intelligence agencies have been warning us about the threat posed by a group known as Al Isabah operating through Twitter and Facebook. The outfit has been trying to link the jihad waged by the ISIS to "Hind, i.e., India – a nomenclature frequently used by Islamic militant groups while referring to India. A video with Hindi subtitles featuring an ISIS spokesman Shaikh Adnani was shown on YouTube and another video displaying the first Friday sermon delivered by ISIS chief Al-Baghdadi, with flawless Tamil subtitles.

Al Isabah Media Production, which claims on its Twitter account to represent the media unit of *"Ansar-ut Tawheed Fi Bilad Al-Hind"* (i.e., supporters of monotheism in India), is responsible for posting these videos. Both Al Isabah's Twitter account and its Facebook page are also linked to other jihadi propaganda, including the link to a book in Hindi titled, *"Jihad Mein Shirkat Ke 44 Tarike"* (44 ways to participate in jihad). The said book, according to some posts on jihadi forums, was purportedly written in Arabic by the since eliminated US citizen-turned jihadi preacher Anwar Awlaki. It was translated into Urdu by one "Abu Haider al-Hindi".

The Facebook page also has several links leading to jihadi literature in Urdu, including a booklet titled, *"Jihad: The forgotten obligation"*, allegedly authored by a radical writer named "Ubaidha al-Hindi".

According to an intelligence sleuth the names Ubaidha-al Hindi and Abu Haider al-Hindi were obviously pseudonyms but were used to project a link to India. Nevertheless, the videos and other materials cannot be taken lightly in view of the reports of Muslim youth from several cities and States rushing to the Caliphate for fighting shoulder to shoulder with ISIS troops.

Al-Baghdadi has been referring to India as the next target in video and audio messages released from time to time. In an audio message released during the month of Ramadan in 2014 Al-Baghdadi claimed that many Indians were part of the ranks of his group and were fighting alongside the Chinese, the American, the French and the German nationals. He has been alleging that India is one of the countries where the rights of Muslims have been forcibly seized. In one of his audio messages Baghdadi criticized the western nations for deliberately ignoring the killings and dismembering of Muslims in Burma, Indonesia and Kashmir.

Consequent upon the formation of Islamic State, several radical outfits based in India are becoming hyper active. It is well known that several Islamic outfits, including the ISIS, Al Qaeda, Indian Mujahideen, all aided by Pakistan, have cast their shadowy web across several parts of India. The shocking chance discovery in October, 2014, of the plot hatched by Jamaat-ul Mujahideen

Bangladesh (JMB) to destabilize West Bengal by staging multiple bomb attacks shows the extent to which the Indian nation has been subverted by multiple Islamic outfits. Occasional incidents of pro-ISIS activities, including distribution of 'T' shirts emblazoned with ISIS flags have been reported from Tamil Nadu – even from Hyderabad and West Bengal.

Within India the teaching of the doctrine of jihad in lakhs of Islamic seminaries, called madarasas, will have a lasting imprint on the minds of young pupils. Several Urdu newspapers have been fanning the fire of hatred and spreading anti-national sentiments among Muslims. For instance, an Urdu newspaper, Akhbar-e-Mashriq, on August 10, 2015, published a news item on its front page proclaiming that the jihadi terrorist, Mohammad Naved, who targeted Udhampur was an Indian – and not a Pakistani. The widely read Urdu newspaper is published from three metropolitan cities, namely Kolkata, Delhi and Ranchi by one M. W. Haque who is based in Kolkata. Many Muslim leaders and Urdu newspapers had openly ascribed the hanging of Yakub Memon, a convict sentenced to death for the 1993 Mumbai bombings, to his being a Muslim. They dubbed it as denial of justice to him. Though the mischievous controversy was started by Assauddin Owaisi, a leader of the MIM (Majlis-e-Itehad-ul Musclemen), the Urdu press kept on targeting the Indian government, the judiciary and the investigating agencies for several weeks in an attempt to provoke the Muslim community against the Indian State. There are many more instances of Urdu newspapers trying to raise communal temperature by provoking the Muslims, almost in the same manner as was done by the Muslim League before the partition of India in 1947.

Faultline Conflicts may Engulf India

The Indian Mujahideen and their fellow travelers planted in India by Pakistan's Inter-Services Intelligence (ISI) are believed to be working in close co-operation with the activists and sympathizers of the ISIS operating underground in India. After subverting Kashmir and penetrating India's vulnerable northeast, the jihadi groups have shifted their focus to south India. In fact, the latest outposts of militant Islam have been set up in the coastal states of Kerala and Tamil Nadu with links in Colombo, the capital of Sri Lanka. Both these States have witnessed a phenomenal growth in the activities of jihadi outfits like Lashkar Tayebba, the Popular Front of India, Al Ummah, the Campus Front and several other militant groups. The ISI of Pakistan has already built the much needed ideological support base in Maldives and developed a toehold in Sri Lanka. They intend to indulge in subversive activities across South India.

The real nightmare for India is likely to surface in the coming decades. The recent revelations by various world media centers confirmed that the ISIS has joined hands with Lashkar-e-Tayeba (LeT).[7] There are reports that the Lashkar has been seeking details of the training programs, beheadings, etc., perfected and practiced by the foot-soldiers of ISIS worldwide. The Caliph of Islamic State has already captured the imagination of a section of Muslim youth in India, Pakistan and Bangladesh.

According to an informed source several new techniques including the use of ambulances filled with detonators might be used by ISIS for staging attacks by remote control. Among other modes likely to be employed for staging spectacular attacks could be trained dogs. Stray animals, including dogs, wearing collars or other contraptions, filled with high grade explosives, may be sent into crowds and then detonated.[8] In furtherance of global jihad all kinds of vile tactics are being considered by ISIS. There are reasons to believe that ISIS, Jaish-e-Muhammad and LeT are working on plans to come together for enhancing their capabilities for future attacks. And they will secure the support of the Inter-Services Intelligence of Pakistan.

Indian Fifth Columnists and Fellow Travelers

Nearly twelve years ago the research undertaken by Sundeep Waslekar's think-tank, Foresight Group, confirmed that by the year 2004 the ISI had successfully set up as many as sixty Espionage Centers all over India in which nearly 10,000 trained spies were employed. Well, that was a rough estimate made by Sundeep Waslekar long ago. Since then much water has flowed down the Ganga. According to reliable intelligence sources by now the number of active ISI-planted espionage centers in India have more than doubled. These espionage centers constitute multiple formidable spy nests of Pakistan's fifth columnists whose activities are growing exponentially. The number of core ISI agents and fellow travelers operating in India is believed to be in the range of fifty to sixty thousand agents or more. They constitute a formidable army whose single-minded mission is to subvert India and Islamize the entire subcontinent by waging Jihad. A number of identifiable pro-jihadi lobbies are operating brazenly, not only in the States, but at all India level too. These traitors and fellow-travelers mostly carry on their mission by masquerading as bleeding heart liberals and preachers of peace and communal harmony. Many of these traitors and fellow travelers, including some politicians, have no shame in openly pleading the cause of jihadi outfits. They constitute a formidable army of fifth columnists whose single-minded mission is to subvert India and Islamize the entire subcontinent by waging the asymmetric war called 'Jihad'.

It may be recalled that according to the deposition made by Mohammed Danish Ansari (an associate of the Indian Mujahideen operative Yasin Bhatkal) in a statement recorded under Section 164 Cr.P.C. by a Magistrate, Yasin Bhatkal had claimed in the year 2010 that he had raised a committed group of 33,000 jihadis in India.[9] The said statement is in possession of the National Investigation Agency.

The disclosure made by Danish Ansari six years ago shows the extent to which the fifth columnists have laid siege to India. A glaring example of the large presence of fifth columnists and fellow travelers in India was that nearly 30 thousand Muslims of Mumbai had joined the namaz-e-janaza at the burial of the notorious terrorist Yakub Memon on 31st July, 2015, who was hanged after his appeal was rejected by the Supreme Court. Due to the threat of lawlessness and to maintain peace in Mumbai the police had to make more than 300 preventive arrests and deploy nearly one thousand personnel to maintain peace. There were huge crowds of mourners at the burial ground. In sharp contrast, the number of Muslim mourners at the burial of the former President of India, Dr. Abdul Kalam, was quite limited, even inadequate. Apparently he was not popular with the Muslim masses. The reasons need not be elucidated !

One of the earliest examples of a highly educated individual taking up arms for an Islamic cause in India was a former surgeon Jalees Ansari of the Tanzim Islah-ul Muslimeen (TIM) which outfit was established in 1985. Ansari had organized a series of bombings in different cities across the country after the demolition of the Babri Masjid in 1991.

Another terrorist Mohammad Abrar Qasim was a dentist before he joined Students Islamic Movement of India (SIMI) in 1993. He used his earnings as a dentist to serve as chief of Bihar's SIMI unit. The activists of SIMI and Indian Mujahideen also set up a Bengaluru cell where at least six IT workers were recruited through a frontline Islamic organization called 'Sarani'. The ace terrorist Mansoor Peerbhoy, who was said to have produced and electronically sent the Indian Mujahideen's manifesto after the 2005 serial blasts in Delhi and elsewhere, was a computer engineer working at Yahoo's Indian office. He was the son of one of the largest wholesale grocery suppliers to the Indian Army's Southern Command.

In 2014, India recorded several incidents of young radicalized Muslims keen to join jihad, several of whom happened to be engineers or engineering students from middle-class backgrounds. The latest tally of ISIS operatives arrested in India is more than fifty-five.

Chapter 6

Conflict Zone India

Ever since independence India has been targeted by multiple Jihadi outfits. Their avowed goal is to Islamize the entire subcontinent. In recent months, however, the jihadi threat has multiplied manifold due to certain geostrategic developments. Consequent upon the formation of Islamic State in Iraq and Syria, the Islamic outfits embedded in India are reported to be preparing for launching multiple terrorist strikes. The battle for the proposed Wilayat Hind project envisioned by the ISIS might start from the state of Jammu & Kashmir in the north and West Bengal and Assam in the east. The coastal State of Kerala is another soft spot. ISIS might take some time for openly targeting India because it is a vast country and an emerging super power. But sporadic spectacular attacks will start sooner or later. When the project becomes operational its reverberations will be heard all over, especially in Maharashtra, Kerala, Karnataka and Tamil Nadu as well.

Indian masses should be alerted that what we are facing is the same jihad which had savaged and ravaged India for more than one thousand years. If the pronouncements of notorious Pak-based jihadis like Hafiz Saeed are to be believed, and some lessons learnt from the brazen attack on Pathankot Airforce Station, we are already in the midst of major faultline conflicts. The danger signals hoisted by the ongoing spurt in aggressive communal politics raging across the

Jawaharlal Nehru University, Indian Institute of Technology, Jadavpur and National Institute of Technology in Srinagar (Kashmir) are straws in the wind. The iron grip of anti-national academia on universities and technical institutions appear to be part of the looming threat of Islam's war of a thousand cuts against India.

The creation of the Caliphate on June 29, 2014, by Al Baghdadi added a new dimension to the geo-religious threat to India. Every militant movement needs a charismatic hero, sort of a high profile role model. At the time of the Russo-Afghan war of 1980s Osama bin Laden had appeared on the scene to lead the Islamic warriors on their long journey. While the long march of Islam has continued all these years, a new Islamic icon Al-Baghdadi has surfaced as the latest warrior of militant Islam.

Indian Youth Joining ISIS

At this stage, it is difficult to estimate how many Indian Muslims will respond to the call of Al-Baghdadi to join the jihad. It is time that Indian strategic analysts undertook a rough assessment of the approximate number of Indian volunteers who may respond to Al-Baghdadi's call for jihad against India. Will their numbers run into thousands or lakhs, no one knows. If the followers of Hindu-hating rabble-rousers like Akbaruddin Owaisi of the Majlis Ittehadul Muslimeen (MIM) and Islamic Research Foundation of Zakir Naik continue to grow, the Indian nation faces the risk of plunging into a civil war like situation.

The phenomenon of Indian Muslims joining the ISIS as jihadis set alarm bells ringing in India's intelligence agencies after the case of Mumbai-based engineering student Areeb Ejaz Majeed, aka Arif Majid, came to light. Initially Majeed was reportedly killed fighting alongside Islamic insurgents in Iraq. The death of 23-year-old Majeed and the online tributes paid to him by the Islamic militant outfit

Ansar-ul-Tawhid hailing his 'martyrdom' confirmed that a section of Indian Muslim youth have been persuaded to lay down their lives "in search of paradise". Later on it came to notice that Majeed had not died fighting for ISIS. Instead he returned to Mumbai.

Prima facie several groups of suspected fifth columnists and fellow travelers are waiting in the wings for lending active support to the ISIS for subverting the Indian nation. Some of them are members of the Students Islamic Movement of India (SIMI) and Indian Mujahideen, several others were associated with Lashkar-e-Tayyeba, Al Qaeda (India Branch), Jaish-e-Muhammad, Al Ummah, Ahle-e-Hadees, All Parties Hurriyat Conference, Dukhtran-e-Millat, Harkat-ul-Jihad-e-Islami, Jammu & Kashmir Islamic Front, Tablighi Jamaat, Popular Democratic Front, Deendar Anjuman, Ansar-al-Tawheed in India, Majlis-e-Ittehad ul Muslimeen and Ansar-al-Tawheed. If the recent events in the JNU are any indication about the shape of things to come, even radical groups like the All India Students Association and Democratic Students Union could be counted as fellow travelers of jihadi outfits working overtime to destabilize India.

Danger Posed by AuT

Animesh Roul, a researcher of the New Delhi-based Society for the Study of Peace and Conflict, has described Ansar-ut Tawheed Fi Bilad Al-Hind, or AuT, as a hitherto lesser known group which publicizes the so-called government atrocities against Muslims in India and urges Indian Muslims to join the Afghan or Syrian jihadi campaigns to mount multiple terrorist attacks inside India. In an article authored for *The Jamestown Foundation's Terrorism Monitor*, Raul pointed out that *AuT* had issued at least four videotapes since October, 2013, including the one on May 17, 2014, calling for attacks against Indian targets worldwide.[1] The ten-minute video featured the AuT leader Maulana Abdur Rahman al-Hindi urging jihadi leaders like Taliban chief Mullah Omar, Al Qaeda's Ayman al-Zawahiri, Caliph Abu Bakr al-Baghdadi, Nasir Abd al-Wuhayshi of Al-Qaeda in Arabian Peninsula, and Al-Shabaab's Abdi Godane to attack Indian government interests and economic centers in India and elsewhere as a means of protecting the Muslims of India.

Earlier this year, the notorious Al Qaeda ideologue Asim Umar had issued a video in Urdu which exhorted Muslims in Jammu and Kashmir and other parts of India to join the jihad being waged by the Islamic State. In one video circulated by Asim Umar a threat to the life of the Indian Prime Minister, Narendra Modi, had been specifically mentioned. One video with Hindi, Tamil and Urdu subtitles, posted on jihadi forums and YouTube, featured a Canadian jihadi named Abu Muslim. He was shown firing a rocket-propelled grenade and participating in combat before being killed. Another video with Hindi subtitles meant for enticing the Muslim youth featured the ISIS spokesman Shaikh Adnani.

The videos and threatening calls posted on Internet can no longer be taken lightly in view of the frequent reports of Muslim youths from Thane, Chennai and Hyderabad travelling to join the ISIS and the arrest of Afshan Jabeen, a woman recruiter from Hyderabad, in October, 2015.

The danger posed by ISIS has to be evaluated with reference to Pakistan's continued attempts to destabilize India by waging the war of a thousand cuts. It may be recalled that the Indian Air Force Station in Pathankot was attacked by a group of Pakistani commandos (called 'fedayeen') on 2nd January, 2016, around 3.30 a.m. They wore military uniforms of the Indian army and were heavily equipped with guns and grenades. It was not a lone wolf target-hit, but a well-planned major attack on an important defense establishment strategically located at a distance of 20 miles from the Indo-Pak border, near Chakki River. The forward airbase has its own Air Traffic control system and a squadron of eighteen MIG-21 fighter jets, a missile battery and quite a few MI-35 helicopters which were sought to be destroyed by attackers.

According to some local residents, the jihadis were shouting, "Allah hu Akbar", "Islamic State Zindabad", "Pakistan Zindabad" etc. They were conversing in the Saraiki dialect of Bahawalpur area which is akin to the Multani language. Incidentally Bahawalpur happens to be the headquarters of Masood Azhar and his anti-India outfit, Jaish-e-Muhammad. Subsequently the attack was traced to the notorious terror outfits Jaish-e-Mohammed and Lashkar-e-Tayebba of Pakistan.

Looking at the perfidy of our wily neighbour there is an urgent need to make a paradigm shift in our response to the repetitive attacks engineered from across the border. An attempt should be made to read the tea leaves of the two jihadi attacks, one targeting a police station in Dina Nagar in the border district of Gurdaspur and the second one at the Pathankot airbase staged within a short period of six months. India must develop the muscle power to hit Pakistan hard, real hard, to pay back the enemy in the same coin. Unfortunately the overall situation continues to be no different from our past, when Hindu leaders failed to unitedly pursue and punish the invaders.

The Indian society suffers from mammoth collective amnesia about the depredations of Muslim invaders for more than one thousand years which led to the slaughter of nearly 8 to 10 million Hindus, as estimated by K. S. Lal, a well-known historian in his well-researched tome, 'Growth of Muslim Population in India'. Unfortunately most Hindus continue to remain inadequately informed about the dangerous ambitions of Al-Baghdadi.

Gravity of the ISIS Threat
In a seminally researched article Tufail Ahmed (an analyst formerly working with the BBC Urdu Service) has highlighted certain key aspects of the threat posed by ISIS to India.[3] According to the information available in public domain the activities of the moles and

sympathizers of the ISIS in more than one dozen states were being watched by intelligence agencies. The main points analyzed by Tufail Ahmed, the present Director of the New York based Middle East Media Research Institute, are discussed below.[3]

- India faces a complicated threat because there is a possibility that the Pakistani military's Inter-Services Intelligence (ISI) could rope in some of the ISIS-affiliated jihadis from Pakistan-Afghanistan region to target India.

- The Indian government should impose stringent curbs on social media networks, as well as on Urdu press, to curtail their pro-jihadi outpourings.

- During the last one year the number of Indian Muslims joining the ISIS and Al-Qaeda, or those expressing support ranged from 5 or 6 to 300. India being a large country with a population of 1.23 billion people, it will be difficult for intelligence agencies to be present everywhere. While the exact figures of Indian Muslims joining ISIS may not be known, it seems that the Indian Muslims attracted to the call of Islamic State could be up to 300.

- Indian Muslims who joined the Islamic State reached the Caliphate through several paths. Four of them flew directly from Mumbai to Iraq. One Kashmiri youth based in Australia went directly to Syria via Turkey, while some Tamil Muslims based in Singapore travelled from there to Syria. Many Indian Muslims from the diaspora in UAE and other Middle Eastern countries too, opted to join the ISIS. Areef Majeed, also referred to as Areeb Majeed, who was one of four Mumbai youths, had disclosed after his return to India that he had counted 13 Indians at a terror training camp in Syria. Also, nearly a dozen Indian Muslims who went to the Pakistan-Afghanistan region are believed to have travelled to the Islamic State.

- Of special concern to India should be the faultline State of Jammu & Kashmir which borders Pakistan. The reports in June – July this year indicated that there has been an increase in support for the ISIS among Kashmiri youths. On June 12, 2015, ISIS flags were hoisted during a protest following the weekly Friday prayers at a mosque in Srinagar as well as at another mosque in Kupwara district. On June 19, 2015, an ISIS flag was waved by a masked youth in a rally organized by separatists in Anantnag district. On June 26, an ISIS flag was waved during a protest in Srinagar. On July 17 and 18, 2016, the flags of ISIS and Pakistan were waved during a protest in Srinagar against the house arrest of secessionist leader Syed Ali Shah Geelani. On July 24, 2015, the ISIS flag was waved in Srinagar. Earlier, Kashmiri youths waved Pakistani flags as a form of anti-India protest. But now the Pakistani flag is being increasingly replaced by the ISIS flag in protests, occuring after the Friday prayers.

- According to reliable sources, the number of foreign terrorists operating in Kashmir is around 50. A journalist, Basharat Masood, wrote in his July 26, 2015 dispatch that 33 young men had joined the ranks of militants in the first six months of the year in the Valley, taking the total number of active militants to 142. Among them nearly 54 were foreigners, mostly from Pakistan.

- Speaking on the Kargil Vijay Diwas, July 26, 2015, Lt. General D. S. Hooda, Indian Army's Northern Command Chief, told reporters that the ISIS was creeping towards India from Pakistan. General Hooda commented that there were no large footprints of ISIS in Jammu & Kashmir, but there were incidents of flag waving which were a matter of concern. Tufail Ahmed further added that during the last one year or so, many Indian Muslims based in Australia and Singapore had allegedly travelled to Syria to join the Islamic State. Four Muslim youngsters from Mumbai flew as pilgrims to

Iraq and then joined the ISIS. Some Indians also travelled to Pakistan-Afghanistan region through the India-Nepal corridor and later joined the ISIS. Some Indian expatriates based in Saudi Arabia, UAE and other Middle Eastern countries too, joined the ISIS. During the last 18 months the number of Indians joining the ISIS has risen to something like 300 to 1000 volunteers.

Urdu Press Needs Curbs

Tufail Ahmed warned the Indian government about the malefic influence of Urdu newspapers and social media on youth. He recommended the need to place effective curbs on the attempts to magnify the so-called grievances of Indian Muslims by the Urdu press and other media outlets, both offline and online. He further emphasized that in India a section of the Urdu press is engaged in supporting the jihadi arguments against democratic governments. Drawing attention to the role of Urdu newspapers in promoting radicalization of Muslim youth, he drew attention to the following instances of inflammatory reporting resorted to by the Urdu press.[4]

Two specific instances of communally provocative writings by India's Urdu press were highlighted by him. The first instance was of a lead article penned by Muhammad Najeeb Qasmi which was published in Roznama *Urdu Times*, a Mumbai-based Urdu daily, in its issue dated December 26, 2014. The article stated that according to the tenets of Islam the killings of Muslims who converted to Hinduism was fully justified. It quoted Hazrat Ayesha, the wife of Prophet Muhammad, saying that the Prophet had laid down that if a person leaves his religion (Islam), then he should be executed. The article was written in the context of the campaign for re-conversion (or ghar wapsi) launched by some Hindu groups for re-conversion of Muslims and Christians. The author, Najeeb Qasmi, quoted certain verses of the Qur'an, some hadiths (sayings and deeds of Prophet

Muhammad), along with the diktats and practices of the righteous Caliphs (the first four Caliphs of Islam - Abu Bakr, Umar ibn Khattab, Usman ibn Affan, and Ali ibn Abu Talib) to justify the killing of apostates. The killing of apostates is a major strategy advocated by jihadi organizations across the world, including Al-Qaeda, the Taliban and ISIS. *The Roznama Urdu Times* emphasized the killing of apostates in following words.[5]

"In this verse (152 of Koran's chapter Al-Araf), Allah has clearly ordered that an apostate be killed... In fact, the first interpreter of the Koran, Prophet Muhammad, has clearly ordered the killing of a person becoming apostate."

The second example cited by Tufail Ahmed was of *Haftroza Nai Duniya*, a mass-circulation Urdu weekly newspaper published and edited by Shahid Siddiqui, a former member of the Indian Parliament. The newspaper's issue dated May 25 – 31, of 2015, was devoted to the problem of 'Terrorism and Islam'. Through a series of articles, whose authors were not identified, the Urdu weekly narrated a number of historical grievances of crimes committed against Muslims, from the time of Prophet Muhammad to contemporary times. The intention was to inflate the anger in the minds of Muslim youth by advancing the arguments which jihadi organizations keep trotting out. The newspaper, Haftroza *Nai Duniya,* further argued that jihad is essentially defensive in nature and that all wars involving Muslims had been started due to aggression on the part of non-Muslims – right from the days of Prophet Muhammad to the present times. By not naming the authors of the articles, *Haftroza Nai Duniya* sought to escape responsibility for the views expressed in the newspaper. The only inference that could be drawn was that those views were of the newspaper's editor, Shahid Siddiqui. The same newspaper also published a provocative conspiracy theory that American soldiers had chopped Osama bin Laden's body into pieces and thrown them off mountains of Afghanistan, while returning from the 2011 operation in Abottabad.

Tufail Ahmed expressed shock on seeing how *Haftroza Nai Duniya* justified the massacre of nearly 900 Jews of Banu Quraiza tribe in the year 627 A. D. in a public square of Medina on the orders of Prophet Muhammad. The Banu Quraiza Jews had surrendered and offered to leave behind their wealth, yet they were assassinated. Tufail Ahmed bluntly asks how an Indian newspaper could justify the massacre of nearly a thousand helpless people and how was he different from the ISIS leader Al-Baghdadi.

Two New Trends

The changing scenario after the events of 2014 points to significant shifts in the mode of recruitment to Islamic terrorist groups from India. Two of these developments are noteworthy. One trend is the fact that more and more Indians were beginning to join global terrorist groups like Islamic State. Their number may be small as of now, but the latest tendency showed an emerging inclination among some Indians to join global jihadi causes. Earlier the distance between the Indian Muslims and the global jihadi outfits was evident in the lack of co-ordination between the cadres of SIMI and Al-Qaeda despite the consistent attempts of the two groups at recruitment from India. The Indian Mujahideen concerned itself primarily with domestic issues and seldom with global jihad. The second departure is the manner in which Internet is being used by the new ISIS terrorists. The IM primarily used internet as a tool for promoting jihad and restricted itself to sending messages to the media, or for communicating with members and for propaganda. But in those days internet was not the only mode of communication and indoctrination. Personal meetings would happen amongst the leaders as well as the recruits. However, in the case of men joining ISIS, all indoctrination and planning is conducted exclusively online.

Dangerous Days Ahead

The Indian Muslim community is 180-million strong. India has the second largest Islamic population in the world. Therefore over the next few years it is likely to become a major source of recruitment for groups like the ISIS, Al-Qaeda and Lashkar-e-Tayyeba. While the number of pro-ISIS youth may be low at present, in the long run this figure could prove to be deceptively misleading. The large Muslim population is bound to be used by the ISIS as a major source of recruitment and radicalization.

Lately Internet has emerged as a powerful instrument for the recruitment and training of the ISIS warriors. India has a fast-growing number of Internet and smartphone users. Increasing numbers of youths are being indoctrinated through propaganda that is freely streaming on Internet. Presently it is the second largest smartphone market in the world and is expected to have a smartphone-user base of over 650 million by 2019. India also has the third-highest number of Internet users in the world. Therefore the possibility of online radicalization gaining wider and deeper ground in the future cannot be ignored.

The success achieved by the ISIS in capturing large territories in West Asia and keeping at bay the western nations by holding on to their gains has made ISIS a more prestigious option for Muslim youth. The fedayeens targeting Charlie Hebdo in France in January 2015, had gunmen linked to Al-Qaeda in the Arabian Peninsula who had transferred their loyalty to Islamic State. Similarly, among the shooters who attacked San Bernardino (California) in November, 2015, at least one had been trained by Al-Qaeda in Pakistan, but over a period of time had shifted his loyalty to the ISIS.

An Islamic State video issuing threats against India was released in the third week of May, 2016, featuring two former members of the Indian Mujahideen. One of the persons identified by the sleuths of the National Investigation Agency was believed to be Mohammad Sajid (also known as 'Bada' Sajid) from Azamgarh in Uttar Pradesh. He was allegedly involved in the serial bomb blasts in Ahmedabad and Jaipur in 2008 and was referring to the Batla House encounter with Delhi Police on September 19, 2008. The second jihadi identified by the National Investigation Agency officers was Abu Rashid Ahmed. He too, was virulently anti-Hindu and proclaimed that his goal was to destroy polytheism and establish Allah's 'nizam' (rule) in India. Rashid who was a former employee of an eye-hospital in Mumbai warned the Indian government that every crime committed against Muslims would be avenged.

Menace of No-Go Zones

The ongoing jihad raging from the USA to the Philippines, constitutes a formidable challenge to the leadership of police and security forces. The global experience is that the growth of jihadi militancy in any State or area is invariably preceded by certain tell-tale marks. The most important signal is the growth of "no-go pockets" where entry of police is resisted. Experiences of the police forces in European countries tell us that these pockets of vexation gradually enlarge into extensive 'no-go' zones which evolve into enclaves of 'vexation and exhaustion' where lawlessness prevails. Very much like Europe, most cities and States in India are now dotted with 'no-go' areas, where neither the Hindus nor the police can enter without facing resistance and violence. This dangerous development in any state, city or town, heralds the growth of under-bed jihadi groups and must be dealt with effectively by police. Across the world, 'no-go' zones are the favorite hideouts of traitors and fifth columnists. Indian cities are no exception. The resistance offered to the police by mobsters controlling the no-go areas facilitates the sheltering of fifth columnists away from the gaze of police and security forces.

India's capital, New Delhi, has a large number of 'no-go' areas. In June 2013 the citizens of Delhi, especially the motorists and pedestrians on Delhi roads had to suffer the harrowing experience of lawlessness throughout the night of the Muslim festival of Shab-e-Barat. The unsuspecting motorists and commuters were caught in a frightful melee caused by thousands of skullcap wearing bikers. Many of them were gesticulating at motorists, especially teasing the lone women car drivers, while performing stunts on the roads of New Delhi. Their rowdy behavior was roundly criticized by the media which faulted the police for the breakdown of public order on the fateful night. These bikers had gathered in a number of 'no-go' areas before racing across the city. The next year, in a desperate bid to prevent the defiant Muslim bikers from creating mayhem on the night of Shab-e-Barat, the Delhi Police went out of their way to seek help of several so-called 'moderate' Muslim leaders, including 21 Imams of various mosques. But their endeavors failed to deter the aggressive bikers. Caring two hoots for the warning issued by the Police Commissioner and unprecedented deployment of police force at nearly 180 strategic points, several determined groups of Muslim bikers came out in a bid to create chaos in the central and south-east Delhi. They tried to create lawlessness in certain Muslim-dominated areas of East Delhi like Seelampur and Usmanpur. Mercifully, the police were able to prevent the bikers from going berserk and challaned nearly 2,000 of them and impounded more than 300 motor cycles. Many roguish bikers could not be caught and challaned on the spot despite the best efforts of the police. There have been sporadic reports of skull-cap bearing bikers trying to create similar lawlessness in other cities like Mumbai and small towns, too. In Delhi and Mumbai gangs of Muslim bikers often gather in 'no-go' areas. During the United Progressive Alliance rule the number of 'no-go' areas in Delhi and several Indian cities grew manifold.

The phenomenon of aggressive Muslim bikers has also surfaced in many other countries, including the USA, U.K. and Australia. On most occasions they ride out of 'no-go' areas. Writing in *The New Media Journal* on January 29, 2013, Soeren Kern, a well-known analyst of the Gatestone Institute, highlighted how Islamic extremists were stepping up the creation of "no-go" areas in several European cities. Many "no-go" zones have been functioning in Europe as Islamic micro-states governed by the Sharia law, highlights the well-known scholar. The governments of the concerned countries have lost control in these areas.

In the United Kingdom a radical group called '*Muslims Against Crusaders*' has launched a campaign to turn 12 British cities, including the national capital, often called "Londonistan" into independent Islamic States. They hope that soon due to sharp rise in Muslim population the so-called Islamic Emirates would start functioning as an autonomous group of Muslim-dominated enclaves ruled by Sharia. One of these so-called Islamic Emirates Project, includes the cities of Birmingham, Bradford, Derby, Dewsbury, Leeds, Leicester, Liverpool, Luton, Manchester, Sheffield, as well as the Waltham Forest area in northeast London and Tower Hamlets in East London as areas marked for enforcing the Sharia rule. In the Tower Hamlets area of East London (also called *Islamic Republic of Tower Hamlets)* Muslim preachers (who refer to it as the Taliban of Tower Hamlets) often issue death threats to women who refuse to wear veils. Soeren Kern points out that many streets have been plastered with posters declaring, "You are entering a Sharia controlled zone: Islamic rules enforced."

In the Finnsbury Park area of Luton, groups of Muslims have been allegedly accused of "ethnic cleansing" by harassing non-Muslims to the extent that many of them have moved out of Muslim-dominated neighborhoods. Soern Kern also draws attention to Leytonstone in East London, where a known Muslim extremist, Abu Izzadeen, publicly heckled the former Home Secretary, John Reid, by asking how dare he enter a Muslim area.

In France, many neighborhoods populated by Muslim are now considered "no-go" zones by the French police. Soeren Kern claims that at the last count there were 751 Sensitive Urban Zones (Zones Urbaines Sensibles) or ZUS, as they are called. That was the number of 'no-go zones' more than three years ago. By now the numbers of these zones has further multiplied. A complete list of ZUS can be found on a website of the French government. It is complete with satellite maps and precise streetwise demarcations. An estimated five million Muslims live in the ZUS territory of France over which the French state has lost control, according to Soeren Kern.

In the capital of Belgium, Brussels (which has more than 25 percent Muslim population), several immigrant dominated neighborhoods like Molenbeek have become "no-go" zones for police officers. They are frequently pelted with rocks by Muslim youth. Interestingly Molenbeek was in the banner headlines news after the 22 March, 2016 attacks in Brussels. In the Kuregem district of Brussels the police are forced to patrol the area with two detachments of police cars. One car is deputed to carry out patrolling while another car follows to protect the first car.

So intense is the fear of Muslim attacks that in the Molenbeek district of Brussels that police officers patrolling the area have been ordered not to drink coffee or eat a sandwich in public during the Islamic month of Ramadan, lest it hurts the sensibilities of Muslims.

In the Netherlands, a Dutch court ordered the government to release to the public, a politically incorrect list of 40 'no-go' zones in the country. The top five Muslim-dominated problem neighborhoods of the country are in Amsterdam, Rotterdam and Utrecht. The Kolenkit area in Amsterdam is considered as the number one no-go "problem district" in the country. The next three districts are in Rotterdam-Pendrecht het, Oude Noorden and Bloemhof. The Ondiep district in Utrecht is in the fifth position among 'no-go'– zones of Netherlands. In Sweden, which has some of the most liberal immigration laws in Europe, large swathes of the southern city of Malmö have become "no-go" zones for non-Muslims and policemen. The city has a 25 percent Muslim population. Though still a minority, they often hold the city to ransom because of their wild ways and deeply aggressive mindset.

The well-researched findings of Soeren Kern about the growth of 'no-go' zone have to be read and understood by Indian police officers in the context of attacks which recently happened in France in November, 2015, and in Brussels in March, 2016. In India, too, multiple terror tactics incidents were witnessed in Burdwan in October, 2014, and more recently in the no-go enclave of Kaliachak in Malda district of West Bengal shaken by riots in the first week of January, 2016.

The real danger posed by the growth of 'no-go' zones in Indian cities lies in the possibility of radical Muslims converting their fortified ghettoes into infamous enclaves of 'vexation and exhaustion' for creating chaos and anarchy. The ideologue of Islamic State, Abu Bakr Naji, has advocated the establishment of such ungovernable spaces as a prelude to the arrival of Islamic State.

Europe Pushed into War Zone

The ISIS attacks in Paris in November, 2015 and again in Brussels in March, 2016, represented a noticeable change in terror tactics. The Paris attacks which killed nearly 132 people while wounding another 350 confirmed that militant groups were now carrying out operations far more sophisticated and difficult to prevent. Since the Madrid bomb blasts of 2004 and the London bombings of 2005 the recent attacks in

Europe moved away from run-of-the-mill bombings, with a high likelihood of failure, and evolved into attacks focused on a combination of suicide bombings, assault weapons and hostage taking. There is a new trend of attacks extending over several days and jihadis targeting multiple locations which are caused by multiple terror cells working in tandem. Further evidence of this was seen on November 18, 2015, when security forces in Paris had to rush to engage the heavily armed terrorists in the northern suburb of Saint-Denis almost five days after the initial attack. The confrontation saw one suspect detonate a suicide vest and others engaging police in a prolonged shootout in what initial reports indicated was a raid on the mastermind of the attacks, Abdelhamid Abaaoud who had come from Brussels.

In a well-researched article posted on the website of *Fair Observer* on 18th November, 2015, Otso Iho, the Lead Analyst at the Intelligence Division of Protection Group International, reviewed the November, 2016 ISIS attacks on Paris. He felt that the mayhem witnessed on 18th November, 2015, indicated a new trend of grit and persistence in the evolution of terror strategy across Europe. According to him, there is a strong possibility of more such attacks in the near future which may be far more difficult to prevent.

The transnational dimensions of the Paris and Brussels attacks are self-evident. These were plotted in Syria, coordinated and organized in Belgium and carried out in Paris and Brussels. This development demonstrates how vulnerable Europe has become to the predatory punches of radical Islam. The attacks, both in Paris and Brussels, required sophisticated information and knowledge sharing, undetected movement of operatives, the manufacture of sophisticated explosive devices most likely in Europe, and the procurement of an arsenal of assault weapons, procured from within Europe. Most notably, the operation was carried out by foreign fighters in a highly alert European security environment, with several of the perpetrators already known to French and Belgian security agencies. The tactics used in Paris, which involved three teams of militants attacking six sites, strongly resembled those used frequently in the war zones of Iraq, Syria, and Afghanistan and even in the Kashmir valley of India.

In the context of attacks in Europe the combining of assault weapons with explosives and hostage taking has enabled militants to enhance the impact of an assault across a city, and then prolonging the attacks from several hours to several days. For instance, although the initial Paris attacks were concentrated around one location on November 13, 2015, several heavily armed jihadis were still being chased, killed and detained five days later. Such tactics tend to divide the security response and increase casualty figures. Earlier, during the January, 2015, attacks on Charlie Hebdo the terrorists had demonstrated the effectiveness of such tactics and highlighted the potential for a much higher death toll than what might have been originally anticipated. Meanwhile Europe has been flooded with thousands of illegal Muslim migrants from Middle East and African countries.

In a bold speech delivered at a meeting of the European Union in November, 2015, Marine Le Pen of the National Front Party, chided the Europeans thus:

> *"If you are unable to name the enemy, you cannot fight the enemy. The assassin is not terrorism. Terrorism is the weapon. The murderer is the ideology of Islamic fundamentalism (in other words, Islam)."*[6]

She further declared, "So, in essence, if we call countries like Saudi Arabia, Qatar, and even Turkey our allies, then we, too, are the allies of Islamic fundamentalism. ... There is no way to screen who is coming into Europe because the Islamic State is issuing valid passports. .... We have no borders and even if we did, we have no military to defend them. That must change or Europe will never be secure." It is a tough warning to all kaffirs, the import of which needs to be understood by Indian strategic analysts and security experts, too.

Fallout of Paris and Brussels Attacks

The attacks in Paris on November, 13, and November 18, 2015, showed adoption of new war zone-style tactics which claimed high casualty rates. But the French security forces, which had since January, 2015 trained to fight Mumbai-style jihadi attacks, fell short of the citizens' expectations. Meanwhile, the Islamic State has been progressing on the learning curve. Future attacks in Europe, America or elsewhere, including India, have the potential to become more deadly. Had any of the three suicide bombers near the spectator-packed *Stade de France* football stadium in Paris managed to enter the match ground, the death toll may have been significantly higher.

Arrests of the perpetrators of the crime and the sources of the weapons and explosive devices used in the attacks have provided further insights into the scale of Islamic State's reach within Europe. Initial findings have already raised concerns over Islamic State's increased capability to orchestrate simultaneous attacks across multiple locations in future. In the week prior to the events in Paris, a man, potentially linked to the attacks, was arrested in Germany in possession of eight assault rifles, three handguns and explosives, while Turkish authorities said they had foiled a major attack in Istanbul allegedly led by a British Islamic State militant Aine Lesley Davis who was involved in planning the Paris attacks.

The attacks in Paris and Brussels will have a long term impact on the life style and security of Christians in Europe. It will restrict their freedom of movement and cause disruption of economic development. On November 17, 2015, for first time in the history of the European Union, the government of France was forced to invoke Article 42.7 of the Lisbon Treaty, which obligates member states to offer France aid and assistance by all means in their power in case of "armed aggression."

In direct response to the transnational nature of the attacks, France announced on November 16, 2015, that it would call for a suspension of Europe's Schengen Agreement, which guarantees freedom of movement within most of the EU nations. Reports that one of the attackers in Paris had entered Greece before traveling to France using a Syrian passport have further fueled concerns over the security implications of the refugee influx into Europe.

Global Muslim Support For ISIS

A new poll by the Pew Research Center revealed significantly higher levels of support for the ISIS in Muslim streets. The poll released in November, 2015, showed that nearly one-third of the Syrian refugees entering Europe were sympathetic to the Islamic State.

The analyst Sierra Rayne pointed out in an article posted on the website of *American Thinker* on 18th November, 2015, the findings of a new poll by the Pew Research Center. It revealed significant levels of support for ISIS within the Muslim world. In eleven representative countries up to 14 percent of the population have a favorable opinion of ISIS and upwards of 62 percent constituted the "don't know" group showing that they had no unfavorable opinion about the Islamist group.[7]

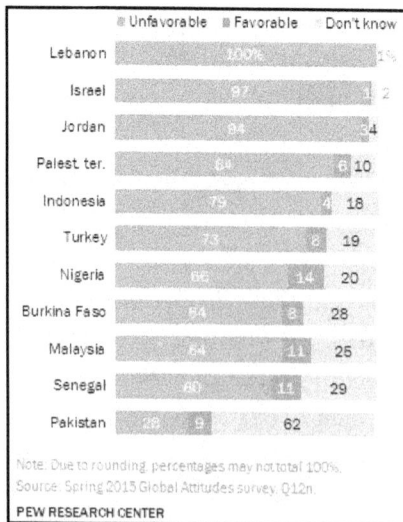

	Unfavorable	Favorable	Don't know
Lebanon	100%		1
Israel	97		2
Jordan	94		4
Palest. ter.	80	6	10
Indonesia	79	4	18
Turkey	73	8	19
Nigeria	66	14	20
Burkina Faso	64	8	28
Malaysia	64	11	25
Senegal	60	11	29
Pakistan	28	9	62

Note: Due to rounding, percentages may not total 100%.
Source: Spring 2015 Global Attitudes survey. Q12n.

PEW RESEARCH CENTER

The survey revealed that in these eleven nation-states alone, the Islamic State has the favorable support of at least 63 million Muslims. The figure could swell to 28.7 million Muslims worldwide, if the undecided were included among the supporters.

Sierra Rayne further highlighted that the Pew poll revealed that in Pakistan, which has nuclear capabilities, only 28 percent of the people viewed ISIS unfavorably and 72 percent Pakistanis were favorably inclined towards Islamic State. Judging by this overwhelming degree of public support in Pakistan, the Islamic State should be considered a proxy nuclear power.[8] Far more shocking details about the fundamentalist mindset of Muslims worldwide were revealed in another Pew Research survey published in *American Thinker* on 11 December, 2015. It warned that the percentages of Muslims favoring the savage practices showed "what the West is up against in the clash of civilizations (or more accurately, World War III)".[8]

Focus on Killing of 'Kaffirs'

An important concern of jihadis during their attacks in Mumbai, Nairobi, Mali and other places, has been to spare the lives of Muslims, and target only the 'kaffirs' or non-Muslims. This vital fact was repeatedly insisted upon by the Pakistan-based handlers of the terrorists who savaged Mumbai on November 26, 2008.

Shortly after Mumbai 26/11 the Israel-based newspaper, *Artuz Sheva,* broke a story which revealed the rabid religious face of the jihad waged by Pakistani Fedayeens and their Pakistan-based handlers. They were repetitively told by their Pakistani handlers to kill only kaffirs and spare the lives of Muslims to the maximum extent possible. This was conclusively proved from important excerpts of the conversation between the fedayeens and their handlers in Pakistan, reproduced by Hana Levi Julian in *Artuz Sheva* and cited in the

Chennai edition of *The Hindu* (sourced from the Israeli newspaper *Artuz Sheva*).[9]

The blood-soaked narrative of the 26 /11 Mumbai carnage and raw savagery of the Pak-trained jihadis did not end there. Santosh Mishra, in his column in *All Mirrors*, Mumbai, reported that jihadis sexually humiliated the guests in hotels before killing them. Disturbing photographs made available to the media by the police vividly showed that several guests at the Taj Mahal Hotel during the siege, were sexually humiliated by the terrorists and then shot dead. Police sources confirmed that even as the terrorists were engaged in a fierce combat with the NSG Commandos, they were humiliating their hostages by disrobing them before ending their ordeal. Eight of the 31 guests killed at the Taj Hotel were foreign nationals. The photographs taken by the police after the hotel was sanitized showed some guests who were in the nude. "Even the Rabbi and his wife at Nariman House were sexually assaulted and their genitalia mutilated," said a senior officer who did not wish to be quoted by name. "We have CCTV footage which revealed how the terrorists forced some of the guests in the restaurants to strip, but there was no evidence of rape," the police officer added.[10]

Yet the Sonia-led previous government and the media, dominated by pro-Muslim anchors and political busy-bodies, continued to fool somnolent Hindus by repeatedly parroting that terrorists have no religion. The truth, however, is altogether different. Terrorists do have a religion and the name of the religion was announced by the Indian Mujahideen in their e-mail of July 2008, forewarning Hindus about their slaughter in Indian cities. The Mumbai 26/11 attack was primarily aimed at targeting the infidels (read Hindus and Jews). Muslims were totally excluded under express orders of the Pakistan-based handlers of fedayeens. Any Muslim killed in a bomb blast or gun attack by jihadis was therefore a collateral damage which the fedayeens could not avoid.

Chapter 7

Islam's Unending War Against Hindus

"Islamic governments have never been and will never be established by peaceful solutions and co-operative councils. They are established, as they have always been, with pen and gun, by word and bullet, by tongue and teeth".

— Preamble of Al Qaeda

It is a pity, nay shame, that even after the globally humiliating mauling of Mumbai by ten Pakistan-trained Commandos on November 26, 2008, we Indians have learnt no lesson. Mumbai 26/11 was tom-tommed as a great achievement by the jihadi outfits operating in Pakistan and Pak-Occupied Kashmir. The audacious attack on the Pathankot Air Force Station on 2nd December, 2015, was yet another feather in the cap of Pakistani outfits targeting India. It led to celebrations by Jaish-e-Muhammad and other Islamic outfits in Pakistan and Pak-Occupied Kashmir. Many Indian politicians, especially those like Mani Shankar Aiyar and Salman Khurshid of the Congress Party and Azam Khan of the Samajwadi party, refused to learn any lessons from the ISIS attacks on Paris on November 13, 2015. Instead of commiserating with the innocent victims they openly justified the dastardly attack on Paris on 13th November, 2015. For these super-secularists the life of a non-Muslim has no value and their political stance is that militant Muslims can do no wrong!

Several months ago the ISIS released a map of the areas which it proposes to take over by 2020, which includes India. In his incisively-researched tome, *'Empire of Fear: Inside the Islamic State'* a BBC Reporter, Andrew Hosken, has published a map of the areas comprising the Islamic world of tomorrow. The map begins with the capture of Andalus (ancient Arabic name of Spain), Portugal, France and the vast lands occupied by the Moors in medieval times. Then it stretches across the Indian subcontinent which, according to Islamic State, would become part of the sub-caliphate named Khorasan. According to Hosken the ISIS have rustled up an army of 50,000 jihadi warriors and seized assets and cash worth two billion dollars after capturing the oil and gas fields in Syria and Iraq.

The growth of ISIS in Bangladesh is undoubtedly a major threat to the security of India. At the same time, the group's attempt to capture Afghanistan constitutes an equally daunting threat to the subcontinent. After their 28th September, 2015, attack on Kunduz the Taliban tried to dominate the geostrategic developments across Afghanistan and Pakistan. For a while the Islamic State receded into the backdrop. In Afghanistan the Islamic State remains engaged in what is best described as a 'tug of war' with the Afghan government as well as the Taliban. Lately, however, there has been a surge in the activities of ISIS in Afghanistan and the Kashmir valley. The Islamic State's propaganda blitz for Wilayat Khorasan has gathered momentum. More videos and handouts have been released during the last few months singing paeans to Wilayat Khorasan than in any other month since inception of the concept. From primary resource documents, the Terrorism Research Analysis Consortium (TRAC) has concluded that the Islamic State has been re-evaluating its objectives in the region. Recently Wilayat Khorasan has started making a forceful push for securing the eastern province of Nangarhar in Afghanistan in a bid to strengthen their influence in the region. The growing focus on

Nangarhar indicates the priorities of Wilayat Khorasan in the region. The influence of Islamic State and Wilayat Khorasan is largely driven by the oxygen gained from the advances made by the group in Iraq and Syria. The Terrorism Research Analysis Consortium has prepared an up-to-date summary of primary material about Wilayat Khorasan. The summary explains the background of the Wilayat Khorasan and the internal dynamics of the militant group. A United Nations report confirmed that ISIS has been winning over a growing number of sympathizers and has been able to recruit followers in 25 of Afghanistan's 34 provinces. The Afghan security forces informed the monitors of the United Nations that approximately ten percent of the Taliban insurgents are ISIS sympathizers. The number of groups and individuals who are openly declaring either loyalty to, or are sympathetic to Islamic State continues to grow. Meanwhile, about 70 battle hardened ISIS Mujahideen are reported to have reached Afghanistan from Iraq and Syria. They constitute the core team of the jihadi fighters. Foreign fighters from Pakistan and Uzbekistan, some of whom have close ties with Al-Qaeda, have joined Islamic State after fleeing their country and have rebranded themselves as ISIS.

Jihadi Maverick Hafiz Saeed

Hafiz Saeed poses a formidable threat to India. He is awfully vicious in thought as well as action. He has been the plotter of several attacks in India, including the Mumbai massacre of 26 November, 2008, and the January, 2016, attack on India's Pathankot air base. Barely three days after ISIS claimed responsibility for the Paris carnage, reports started pouring in of likely attacks on Indian cities by Islamic outfits. The threats came from posts on Internet and social networking sites espousing the extremist ideology.

The praise lavished on ISIS by Hafiz Saeed in a public rally in December, 2014, is a pointer to the future developments in the subcontinent. It confirms the strong possibility of collaboration between India-based terror groups like Indian Mujahideen, Hurriyat Conference, the United Jihad Council and multiple outfits operating from Pakistan with Islamic State. According to intelligence agencies the most vulnerable areas in the country are Maharashtra, Andhra Pradesh, Telangana, Karnataka, Tamil Nadu, Kerala and West Bengal. These might be targeted by ISIS.

ISIS Rising in Maldives

A failed Indo-US operation to stop a radicalized Maldivian family of 12 members from flying out from Bengaluru in December, 2015, to join the Islamic State in Syria has brought into focus the worrying trend of jihadis using India as a transit point and the danger of a perilously-close island nation turning into a hotbed of extremism.[1] The Island State of Maldives has been morphing into an operational station for the Islamic State. On 13th December, 2015, a team of Mumbai police went on a hot chase to intercept a family of twelve Maldivians traveling post haste to the Islamic State. The secret operation lasted nearly 100 hours involving a team of Mumbai police. The unsuccessful pursuit was called off after the twelve ISIS supporters managed to get on a Qatar Airways flight QR 673 to Istanbul (Turkey) via Doha on December 13, 2015. They were tracked to Istanbul on 13 January, 2016.

The runaway Maldivian family was of special interest to the US because one of them, Abdulla Mubarak, is a certified pilot from Miami Federal Aviation Administration Department and could be used for a 9/11-type operation by ISIS. For India, the threat is of long-term nature due to the risk of a neighboring country turning into an outpost of the Islamic State. The family had landed in Bengaluru on December 7, 2016, on a health visa and their eventual exit would have gone unnoticed, if the US intelligence agencies had not alerted their

Indian counterparts. It sparked off a chase that was monitored in two countries by multiple agencies. The migrating family had kept some of India's senior most police officers and intelligence sleuths on their toes. The Police Commissioner of Mumbai, Datta Padsalgikar, confirmed on 21 April, 2016, the news of the Maldivian family transiting via Bengaluru to West Asia, but declined to provide the details due to the on-going investigations.

Though the family entered India on medical visas, the investigating teams found that none of them ever visited any hospital or medical facility.[5] Five members of the family from the Gaaf Alif Atoll, Kondey Island, Male were allegedly radicalized by a Male-based organization called *Jamiatul Salafi*. They have been identified as Abdulla Mubarak (the trained pilot) 30; Muizz Hasan 28, Ahmed Azmeer 32, Zoona Zareer 27, and Zahida Zareer 30. They arrived in India by Air India flight AI 266 on 13 December, 2015.

According to a rough estimate, more than 150 Maldivians have already joined the ISIS and have become a part of the extremist organization Al Hind Brigade. Maldives lies to the southwest of India and close to Sri Lanka. It has a small population of four lakh inhabitants, mostly Muslims. Till a few years ago the Maldivians looked at India as a good neighbour. But the sentiment has changed in recent years. Radical Maldivians now look at India as kafir harbi – the warring nation of infidels who have to be subdued. The very title of the jihadi group comprising Maldivians, captioned 'Al Hind Brigade', confirms that the radicals recruited by ISIS were being trained to target the Indians.

Prophet's Black Flag

In a latest e-book titled '*Black Flags from the Islamic State*', the ISIS warned the faithful living in non-Muslim countries that they were being considered enemies by the majority non-Muslim population ever since the birth of the Islamic State.[2] Therefore it has become imperative for all Muslims to join the global jihad against kaffirs.

Among other things, the e-book released by the Islamic State online, has made a direct reference to the Indian Prime Minister Narendra Modi, describing him as "a right-wing Hindu nationalist who worships weapons and is preparing his people for a future war against Muslims". But erroneously the terror organization mentioned our Prime Minister Narendra Modi as "President Narender Modi of India". This e-book is essentially a compilation of the history of the ongoing jihad and its transformation from Al-Qaeda to the Islamic State. It is largely based on the writings in the online magazine *Dabiq*.

The ISIS has vowed to expand its holy war against India, citing 'apocalyptic religious prophecies' which forecast a global war that will precede the 'return of the Mahdi', or redeemer, who will rid the world of kaffirs and pave the way for the Day of Judgment. "The Islamic State would now expand beyond Iraq and Syria", the book, *Black Flags* declares ominously. It promises to expand into India, Pakistan, Bangladesh, Afghanistan and several other countries to battle the kaffirs. It may be recalled that Prophet Muhammad used to fly a 'black flag' adorned with 'Shahida' (or Kalma) written across in white print. The adoption by the ISIS of the black banner of Prophet Muhammad has special significance for devout Muslims across the world. It imparts strength to their resolve to accomplish the ultimate victory of Islam over heathens. According to one Hadith the Prophet had prophesied that an armageddon of black flag carrying jihadi soldiers from Khorasan will defeat and destroy the kaffirs of Hind (Hindus of India) and then proceed to West Asia.

Tough Training Regimen for Jihadis

The theory and practice of the ISIS prescribes an overwhelming emphasis on physical fitness and training of the Mujahideen to shape them into hardy fighters. It is considered the most important component of jihad. The book prescribes exceptionally high standards of physical fitness and combat efficiency for youth opting to sign up for Jihad. The rigorous standards of physical fitness are described below.

1. Jog for 10 kilometers (about 6.2 miles) without stopping, and this should take the warrior no more than 70 minutes in the worst of cases.

2. Run a distance of 3 kilometers (roughly 2 miles) in about 13.5 minutes.

3. Run for a distance of 100 meters with only 12-15 seconds of rest in between.

4. Walk a long distance without stopping once for at least 10 hours.

5. Carry a load of 20 kilograms (around 44 pounds) for at least 4 hours straight.

6. Perform at least 70 pushups in one shot without stopping (one can start by performing 10 pushups at once, then increasing the number by 3 every day until eventually reaching 70).

7. Perform 100 sit ups in one shot without stopping (one can start by performing 10 sit ups at once, then increasing the number by 3 every day until eventually reaching 100).

8. Crawl using arms for a distance of 50 meters in 70 seconds at most.

9. Perform the 'Farrata' like run (an exercise that combines speed walking, jogging and running) the drill for which as follows:

   a) The Mujahid begins by walking normally for 2 minutes, then he walks quickly for 2 minutes, then he jogs for 2 minutes, then he runs for 2 minutes, then he runs fast for a distance of

100 meters, then he returns to walking, and so on and so forth until he performs this exercise 10 times non-stop. Normal walking differs from quick walking, which differs from jogging, which differs from running. Normal walking is known to all, while quick walking is where one walks at a greater speed while making sure not to raise his feet from the ground for a greater amount of time than he would while walking normally.

b) As regards jogging, a Mujahid is required to cover a distance of one kilometer (roughly 0.6 miles) in less than 5.5 minutes. As for running, it is necessary for everyone to cover a distance of one kilometer in less than 4.5 minutes, etc.... (The book, '*The Black Flags*', pp. 9-10)

Bomb-Making Formula

To give impetus to the cult of car bombings by Jihadis against non-Muslims the ISIS e-book disseminated the process to all Muslim outfits in their online venture. Page 74 of the e-book provides detailed instructions on how various cells of the Mujahideen should work together to manufacture and use car bombs to kill the enemies (kaffirs). They are advised to follow the drill elucidated below:

1. Cell No. 1 makes or gets its own bomb making materials (explosive powder) from the black market and delivers it at a hidden drop off point (possibly even burying it underground). They will leave a secret mark there to show that the material has been placed and will send a secret letter/message to members of Cell 2 to show it has reached desired location.

2. Cell No. 2 will find out if the equipment is ready and go secretly to pick it up. They will then take it to their Garage which looks like a normal garage but is being used undercover by Mujahideen for jihadi activities. Here they will put the explosive powder

(usually fertilizer powder mixed with diesel [Technical name: Ammonium Nitrate + Fuel Oil = ANFO]) in metal steel boxes and insert wires/detonating cables in the boxes. When the fertilizer powder and diesel are ignited (by the naked wires) they suddenly explode. In a normal car bomb, there is usually 1 tonne of ANFO. The ANFO explosive powder metal boxes might be inserted in the boot and bonnet of the car, or wherever there is a gap.

3. Cell No. 3 will be informed through a secret letter or human messenger (courier) that the equipment (car bomb) is ready and if they need it, they can pick it up from a private location which they have already decided between themselves. For this purpose Cell 3 might have members who are willing to undertake the martyrdom operations (suicide bombings). So the leader of Cell 3 will inform one of his men to pick up the car from the secret place and bring it to the martyrdom operator. The martyrdom operator will then drive the car to a place where a number of the enemies have gathered and press the button (Arabic name Doqma). A full electric circuit will be made by the button-press, and electricity will pass through the detonating wires to ignite the main explosive powder (ANFO) in the metal boxes. One tonne of ANFO will explode, ripping through the entire car, killing the martyrdom operator and all the enemies surrounding the car.

4. Each Cell will contain around 5 members each, communicating through secret messengers. These messengers will speak to the leader of the other Cell and no-one else. These secret communications make it harder for Intelligence agencies to know the secret of Cell groups because only one designated messenger communicates between 2 Cell leaders, and no-one else knows the secrets of other Cells.

According to the e-book, the above mentioned techniques should be used by the Mujahideen to transport weapons, to organize fighters and for sending money and supplies to each other while waging jihad. By recourse to killings and bombings the ISIS wants to accomplish its goal of destroying all non-Muslim civilizations worldwide. By imparting rigorous training to the Mujahideen and recourse to limitless savagery, the ISIS wants to accomplish its goal of annihilating all non-Muslims from this world.

In the e-book titled, *Black Flags from Islamic State*, ISIS has propounded its theory of waging jihad against all kaffir regimes and outlined the methodology for stepping up the jihad. For waging this holy war, detailed instructions have been given to Islamic warriors for the creation of covert cells, the formulae for manufacturing explosives and the maintenance of operational secrecy to defeat surveillance by security agencies. The Islamic State's strategic book *Black Flags*, advocates adoption of "hit-and-run tactics and then go into hiding so that the world can waste millions or billions of Euros on 100,000 plus police investigators, and shuts down its major cities. That will make the kaffirs lose tons of money." It gleefully notes that the November 2015 terror shutdown cost Belgium Euros 53 million per day. That was the money spent on hunting down 20 warriors of Islam who were equipped with AK-47 rifles which cost a few thousand dollars. The e-book warns that the future attacks, will make some kaffir groups in the West counter-attack Islam, as a result of which the Muslims in Europe will be forced to pick up guns and start fighting to defend themselves. Then a jihad will begin in Europe too, just like it did in Syria and Iraq. For that eventuality the book *Black Flags,* provides guidance to the faithful.

To meet the challenge of Islamic State India will have to devise a long-term plan to outsmart the jihadi warriors. Indian strategists will have to re-train our security personnel to outmatch the tough training regimen and combat efficiency of ISIS warriors. It needs to be understood that in the chequered history of India the jihadi onslaught has been a never-changing *constant*. Sooner or later, perhaps sooner than later, Islamic State will mount a multi-pronged attack on India which might commence with lone wolf attacks. The creation of Wilayat Khorasan and the focus on project Wilayat Hind are straws in the wind which predict the direction of the rising Islamic maelstrom. Multiple attacks will come from outside as well as inside. Therefore, time has come for Indian security experts to prepare a rough estimate of the likely number of Indians who might respond to Al-Baghdadi's call for jihad against India. At this stage no one can guess whether their numbers will run into thousands or lakhs.

Hindus Ordered to Accept Islam or Die

Last year a 22-minute video was circulated by Islamic State, calling upon the Hindus either to convert to Islam or prepare to be slaughtered. Released on Friday 20th May, 2015, the video features Indian jihadis who have joined the global jihad. It is meant to convince their "brothers" in India to stop living among Hindus and forbids trading with the kaffirs. It has also has allegedly directed Indian Muslims to kill their Hindu neighbors – a strategy which could lead to eruption of religion-based faultline clashes in cities and towns.

Among other things, the video also showed the faces of several still-to-be-identified members of the ISIS. Some of them are suspected to be erstwhile activists of the Indian Mujahideen who are believed to have joined the Islamic State after breaking away from their Pakistan-based leadership. The language used is a mixture of Pushto and Arabic with a smattering of English. An English speaking jihadi says that Hindus in India have three options: *"Accept Islam, pay Jizya, or prepare to be slaughtered"*. The video also talks about horrific atrocities allegedly committed against Muslims, and asks the latter to stop following the ways of the West. It exhorts the faithful to leave their professions as doctors or engineers and join the cause of the Caliphate.

An engineering student from Thane in Maharashtra, Fahad Tanvir Sheikh, who travelled to Syria in 2014 along with three other men from the city, is the only individual conclusively identified in the video, in which he uses the pseudonym Abu Amr' al-Hindi. *"We will return,"* Sheikh Fahid vows, *"but with a sword in hand, to avenge the Babri Masjid, and the killings of Muslims in Kashmir, in Gujarat, and in Muzaffarnagar."*

The video begins by showing Muhammad bin Qasim's conquest of Sindh, claiming that he laid the foundations for Islamic rule in India. Large parts of the video, narrated in Arabic, seek to provide context to the presence of Indian jihadis in the Islamic State. They describe themselves as jihadis from *"Hind wal'Sindh"*, a common term used for volunteers from India and Pakistan. Explaining his personal journey, one jihadi claims that he was forced to leave Mumbai for the Khorasan region, or the Afghanistan-Pakistan borderland, after the 2008 shootout at Batla House, in which Indian Mujahideen commander Atif Amin was killed. This first hijrat, or religious migration, was followed by a second one to Syria, the man recounts. He vows to return to avenge atrocities against Muslims in India.

Another recruit warns Indian Muslims that Hindus are trying to convert them to their faith. The video consists of interviews, mainly conducted at an unidentified coastal location. There is no combat footage of Indians, barring one sequence involving several men in two boats, first released by the Islamic State's Indian affiliate, *Junod Khilafat-al-Hind*, last year.

The jihadis interviewed also praised the quality of life in the Islamic State. "Here there is shari'a in Islamic State," one jihadi says. "Here the hands of thieves are cut off. Here, our religion is safe." The video assails mainstream Muslim politicians and clerics for compromising with what the narrator describes a tyrannical system responsible for massacring Muslims. Images of the Majlis-e-Ittehad-ul-Muslimeen leader Assaduddin Owaisi and All India United Democratic Front politician Badruddin Ajmal are juxtaposed with dead bodies of victims of communal riots. The most acidic invectives, however, are reserved for Islamic clerics of India who, the video alleges, have been supporting the forces of kuffar against the Mujahideen of the Islamic State.

Do not listen to those who tell you that Islam is a religion of peace, an Indian Jihadi Abu Salha al-Hindi, asserts, *"Islam was never a religion of peace for even one day. Islam is a religion of war"*. The Prophet commanded us to remain at war until the day the rule of Allah is established, he asserted.

Many members of Indian Mujahideen are known to have travelled to Islamic State-held territory from 2014 onwards, after rejecting the leadership of their Karnataka-born chief Riyaz Bhatkal. These included the Mumbai hospital employee Abu Rashid Shahnawaz Ahmad, a Unani doctor and son of a local politician of the Samajwadi Party in Azamgarh district of Uttar Pradesh. Others who migrate included two students : Mohammad 'Bada' Sajid and Mirza Shadab Beig. Muhammad Shafi Armar from Karnataka, formerly of the Indian Mujahideen, has been named by the National Investigation Agency as a key suspect in several recent cases relating to Islamic State.

Interestingly, on 22 May 2016, the *Sunday Times of India,* New Delhi, had frontlined the story of an army wife complaining that she was unable to rent a house because she was a Muslim.[3] The disheartened lady lamented that house owners refused to rent out their houses to her when they learnt about her religion. The newspaper flashed the story in four columns, spread over two pages, but without caring to ascertain the fears of house owners and their viewpoint. It appeared to be a typical trick of the trade adopted by the self-styled secular journalists to misrepresent the ground situation. The complaint of the army wife should have been assessed in the light of the diktat issued by ISIS directing Muslims to kill their Hindu neighbours. It needs to be understood that due to the fear and fright created by the attacks of Islamic militants not many non-Muslim house-owners will be willing to stick their necks out. Another aspect of the problem, ignored by most columnists and telemedia anchors, is that due to repeated jihadi attacks the memory of past atrocities committed by Muslim invaders for subjugating the so-called kaffirs has been revived. That has led to widening of the historical divide between Hindus and Muslims in recent years.

The challenge posed by savagery practiced by Islamic State is real. The Indian defenders being unable to run toe to toe with Islamic savagery must master the Israeli technique of massive retaliatory strikes against the enemy. Inflicting higher military and civilian costs is the only answer to the Islamic doctrine of gross savagery. In the coming decades, reliance on steel and steely resolve alone will safeguard the Hindu identity of India.

For centuries jihad has been fine tuned into a comprehensive strategy of war waged against non-Muslims by multiple means. A candid analysis of the doctrine of jihad and its application for terrorizing the infidels was presented by the retired Pakistani Brigadier S.K. Malik of Pakistani army in his tome, *The Quranic Concept of War*, the Foreword of which was written by late General Zia-ul-Haq, a former military dictator of Pakistan. According to Brigadier Malik, jihad is a never ending war for establishing the supremacy of Islam, waged on all fronts including political, economic, social, psychological, moral and spiritual. He has cited several ayats from the Quran emphasizing why and how jihad has to be waged against infidels by recourse to terror. Anyone carefully reading Brigadier Malik's book will realize that what ISIS is doing in West

Asia, Africa, Afghanistan and Bangladesh is not mere terrorism. It is jihad proper, raw and gory in its medieval manifestation.

Training Centres of ISIS

There are reasons to believe that Islamic State has started establishing training centers in certain vulnerable parts of India. Yasmin Ahmad, a 28-year-old school teacher in Kerala was recently arrested on the ground of being a suspected ISIS recruiter. She told the investigators that a person called Abdul Rashid, an ISIS recruiter, held training classes in Kerala. He is now operating out of Afghanistan.[4] The woman recruiter made sensational revelations before the Special Investigation Team of Kerala Police that the Iraq and Syria based global terror outfit is secretly running terror classes in Kerala where 40 people have been indoctrinated in the ideology of jihad.

The lady was arrested at the Delhi airport in first week of August, 2016, before she could board a flight to Kabul. She was going to join Abdul Rashid there. Her friend Rashid is believed to have managed the disappearance of 21 youth from Kerala in the months of May and June, 2016. Yasmin Ahmad couldn't go along with the group of 21 jihadis due to a problem with her 4-years old child's travel documents. She belongs to Saudi Arabia and had come to Kerala three years ago after finding a job in Peace International School in Malappuram. There she met Rashid who used to conduct sessions in the garb of Quran classes. In reality he would brief the recruits about the Islamic State. He regularly read the ISIS magazine, Dabiq, and used material from online propaganda to indoctrinate the youth. It is reasonable to presume that ISIS might have set up similar training centres in other States also.

It needs to be understood that the total sum of ISIS presence in India is far higher than the numbers believed to be embedded across various States. To know the approximate number of Indian volunteers joining Islamic State a State-wise check-list should be prepared by intelligence agencies. There are reasons to believe that the number of radicalized Muslim youth in India runs into thousands. The huge following of Zakir Naik across India indicates that the number of radicalized youth could as well run into several lakhs ! Colossal damage to India's unity was done by the preachings of 25,000 Wahabi scholars and Maulanas from foreign countries who were allowed to have a free run in the country in 2013, as pointed out by Prof. Saroj Kumar Rath, in his analysis.

To sum up, the Indian leadership will have to re-draw and implement an effective training programme for defence services and police forces. Unremitting savagery was the most important arrow in the quiver of the Islamic invaders in the past. It continues to be the *modus operandi* of the jihadi militants led by their self-proclaimed Caliph.

Chapter 8

Battling the Barbarians

"We will return, but with a sword in hand, to avenge the Babri Masjid, and the killings of Muslims in Kashmir, in Gujarat, and in Muzaffarnagar."

– Fahad Tanvir Sheikh
(Codename Abu Amr' al-Hindi)

Before the Mumbai massacre of 26 November, 2008, the Indian Mujahideen had served notice of their intent to kill Hindus. The warning was issued by the militant groups by circulating an e-mail in July, 2008, directing Hindus to either accept Islam or get ready to be slaughtered in Indian cities. Unfortunately the central government did not alert the unsuspecting citizens about the threat issued by the Indian Mujahideen. No wonder, not only Mumbaikars, even the Mumbai police were caught unawares.

The myopic policy of the UPA government chaperoned by Sonia Gandhi, tried to conceal the truth about the intentions of jihadis and the decision of Dr. Manmohan Singh to not alert the public to brazen threats, was responsible for heavy toll of life in the Mumbai massacre. Deliberate concealment of the warning given to Hindus by Indian Mujahideen through their two e-mails of November 2007 and July 2008, can be interpreted only in the context of the UPA's vote-bank politics. The ruling duo miserably failed to alert the Hindu masses about the contents of the Indian Mujahideen's e-mails, repeatedly calling upon Hindus either to convert to Islam or be massacred just as their forbears were by Muhammad bin Qasim, Mahmud Ghaznavi and Muhammad Ghori. The warnings by e-mails sent by the Indian Mujahideen – not just one or two, but five, made their intentions quite clear. It is anybody's guess whether the silence of the then ruling United Progressive Alliance leaders was occasioned by their dhimmitude, or by vote bank politics! In any case, the government failed to alert the nation, well in time. Rest is history.

Defeating ISIS

Some western experts claim that it is not difficult to destroy the ISIS by doing what was done to Germany during World War II by massive carpet bombing of Dresden. At that time the exceptionally high level of destruction was deemed necessary before the allied armies could march into Germany. But those were different times and the concept of avoiding collateral damage to innocent citizens was not popular in 1945. The nuclear attacks on Hiroshima & Nagasaki were justified by advancing the plea of avoiding large scale US casualties that would have occurred during the impending invasion of Japan. But the global mindset today is altogether different from that of 1945.

There is, however, a possibility that a nation like Russia might one day opt to confront the Islamic State head on. One has to just look at what the Russians did to the city of Grozny in the years 1999-2000. The war against Islamic insurgents in Chechnya was won by Putin by using ultra-smart tactics combined with a brutality that out-matched the savagery of the Chechens. The strategy worked well and succeeded. It also led to Russia's resurgence. It is felt by some strategists that Putin might decide at a future date that the war against ISIS needs to be treated like an extension of the Chechen conflict. The

Russians have shown greater interests for protecting their interests and displayed a stronger will to vanquish ISIS than what has been displayed by President Barack Obama. That explains why the French President Hollande expressed his inclination to cooperate with Russia in his war on ISIS. He has discovered that, unlike Barack Obama, Vladimir Putin of Russia plays the war-game better.

Major Obstacles to Defeating ISIS

A big obstacle to the defeat of the Islamic State is that no Muslim country of West Asia genuinely considers ISIS as its main enemy. Saudi Arabia and most Gulf countries, America's vaunted allies, consider Iran as their primary enemy. They regard ISIS as a useful counter against Iran's ambition to dominate Syria and Iraq. Ultimately, however, even Saudi Arabia will be eclipsed.

If western powers fail to stop the ISIS juggernaut rolling towards Afghanistan, Pakistan and Bangladesh, the Indian State might have to join the battle. In such a scenario a major obstacle to stemming the tide will be the presence of a large number of pro-jihadi political parties and the supporters of jihadi outfits embedded across our country. A large number of them are sympathetic to the idea of destroying Hinduism. A point which Indian policy makers must understand is that the ISIS is only a symptom of the deep-rooted militant malady which had gave rise to Al Qaeda before the emergence of Islamic State. The same militant ideology led to the partition of India in 1947. Thus the Frankenstein of Jihad against India has come alive, once again, in the shape of the ISIS!

Combating Islamic Savagery

To meet the challenge of brutality posed by the Islamic State it is essential to devise multiple strategies. India's chequered history of fighting the Islamic invaders shows that in medieval times, Sikh warriors like Hari Singh Nalwa, Dewan Mohkam Chand and Jassa Singh Ahluwalia were successful in defeating the savagery of alien invaders by displaying raw grit and unbounded spirit of sacrifice. The motto of the Khalsa warriors like Hari Singh Nalwa was 'ask for no mercy from savages, nor give any quarter to them'. Ultimately the Sikh warriors won. In modern times the use of savagery as a force-multiplier has been successfully check-mated only by the Israelis from whom we Indians have to learn a great deal.

History is a loud witness to the use of savagery as a most vicious tool by Emperor Jahangir for murdering the fifth Sikh Guru Arjan Dev in a brutal manner. The epitome of spirituality and a saint with rare courage, Guru Arjan Dev was made to sit on a hot plate by the orders of Moghul emperor Jahangir and hot sand was poured on him to torture him to death. The ghastly murder of Guru Arjan Dev in June 1606 at the age of 42 had a long term impact on the opposition to Muslim rule and the consequential militarization of the Hindus of Punjab. In 1699 the great Guru Gobind Singh created the Khalsa at Anandpur Sahib to fight the Islamic tyrants and freebooters.

Later on Aurangzeb, the cruelest of all the Mughal kings, not only tortured and beheaded Guru Tegh Bahadur along with his braveheart disciples, but was also responsible for killing the four gallant sons of Guru Gobind Singh. Two elder sons of the great Guru, Sahibzade Ajit Singh and Jujhar Singh, attained martyrdom in 1704 during the battle of Chamkaur Sahib, while the two younger sons, Sahibzade Fateh Singh and Zorawar Singh, were bricked alive in 1705 at Sirhind, under the orders of Aurangzeb. Bricking alive children of a tender age was a typical example of the gross savagery practiced by Muslims.

The burden of the worst Islamic savagery was, however, borne by Guru Tegh Bahadur, his gallant son Guru Gobind Singh himself, and his famous disciple, Banda Singh Bahadur. The famous warrior Banda Bahadur was arrested on December 17, 1715, along with thousands of Sikh soldiers, by Samad Khan, the Mughal Subedar of Punjab, after an eight-month long siege of Fort Gurdas Nangal in district Gurdaspur. The starved Khalsa soldiers, emaciated by hunger, were defeated in a fierce battle between the beleaguered Sikhs led by Banda Bahadur Singh and the huge army of the Muslim ruler, Farukhsiyar.

According to the narrative of Sikh valour recorded in Indian history, after being defeated Banda Bahadur was imprisoned in an iron cage, and hundreds of Sikh soldiers were chained and menacled while being brought to Delhi. The intensity of terror unleashed by the Muslim ruler can be assessed from the fact that the defeated Banda Bahadur accompanied by 700 captive Sikh soldiers, along with heads of 2000 Sikhs impaled on spears of Mughal soldiers and 700 cartloads of slaughtered Sikhs, were paraded through the streets of Delhi to terrorize the population.[1] They were imprisoned in the Delhi fort and tortured for many days in a bid to convert them to Islam. But true to the Sikh tradition of the saffron-colored sacrifice, all of them refused to convert to Islam. Thereafter, for seven days one hundred Sikh soldiers were brought out of the fort every day and publicly slaughtered. Yet no Sikh opted for conversion, nor gave up his faith. On June 9, 1716, Banda Bahadur's eyes were gouged out, his limbs were severed, his skin was peeled and he was killed in the cruelest possible manner, under orders of the Mughal king, Farukhsiyar.[2] The Islamic savagery was countered by the unflinching resolve of the Sikhs to win. Ultimately the gallant fight by the Sikh warriors in Punjab and the rise of Marathas in the central and South India put paid to the savagery of Islamic rulers. Even after being defeated by Ahmed Shah Abdali in the third battle of Panipat in 1761, the Maratha warriors rose again with double vigour to pursue the invading tyrants, right up to the shores of the Indus River.

In modern times the savagery of Islamic soldiers has been defeated solely by the strategists of the Israeli army and no other nation. Israelis have been able to stem the tide of Islamic onslaught by their policy of quick attrition which tends to impose heavy costs on the aggressors. It is done by the use of latest technology and weaponry – laced with raw courage. The Israeli narrative of gutsy battles with Islamic militants and repelling their onslaughts by imposing heavy costs has become a legend. It needs to be studied by the Indian strategists.

Listen To Tony Blair

Time has come for Indians strategists to listen to Tony Blair, the former British Prime Minister. He delivered a keynote speech on 23 April, 2014, at Bloomberg headquarters in London on the subject 'Why the Middle East Still Matters'. Blair spelt it out in no uncertain terms that presently radical Islam posed the greatest threat to the world.[3] According to him there are four reasons why Middle East remains the prime geo-political concern. The first three, namely the oil, the region's proximity to Europe and the role of Israel were quite important, but these were not the focus of Blair's speech. He rapidly moved to the fourth and the most important reason, namely, Islamic extremism. According to him the conflict in the Middle East was between an open and tolerant society and the fundamentalist Islamic ideology. He commented that "wherever you look – from Iraq to Libya to Egypt to Yemen to Lebanon to Syria and then further afield to Iran, Pakistan and Afghanistan – this is the essential battle."

Addressing members of the civil society who often disregard or try to minimize the likely consequences of such conflicts, Blair observed that there was something odd about the reluctance to accept what is so utterly plain, namely their common struggle around the issue of the rightful place of religion, and particularly of Islam, in politics. He hammered home this aspect of Islam again and again during his forty minute speech and warned that the struggle will not end at the borders of the region. The real threat, according to him, was that this ideology was being exported around the world. The former

Prime Minister of the United Kingdom advised the audience to analyze the world situation today.[4] There is no region of the world, not adversely affected by Islamism, he emphasized. His speech focused on two peculiar aspects of jihadi Islam. The first aspect, according to him, is a deeply rooted desire on the part of western commentators to analyze these issues as disparate events. They keep on arguing that this threat is not really about Islamic ideology. They adduce the plea that there could be some local or historic reasons which might explain what is happening. There is an attempt to ignore the obvious common factor, in a manner that is almost willful.

Blair further pointed out that the second aspect of the problem was a deep desire to separate the political ideology represented by groups like the Muslim Brotherhood from the actions of extremists. The motivation behind these fears is that if one tried to identify it truthfully one will be accused of being anti-Muslim, a sentiment on which the Islamists cleverly try to play. He pin-pointed the profound danger posed by the radical ideology and concluded that Islamic preaching was incompatible with the modern world. He therefore urged the West and indeed the entire world to unite against the growing ideology of Islamic extremism.[5]

Blair reminded the audience that the Muslim population in Europe had grown to more than 40 million and was still growing. He alleged that the Muslim Brotherhood and other radical outfits were increasingly active and they were able to operate without being investigated.

Need For Boots on Ground
It is claimed that the American air strikes have killed nearly 25,000 fighters of Islamic State. But the success of incessant aerial bombings by the Western powers and Russia has not been able to stop the expansion of ISIS militants into Europe, North Africa and nearer home, into Afghanistan and Bangladesh. The spectacular attacks in

Paris, Brussels, Jakarta, Istanbul, Lahore, Dhaka and Quetta show the steady forward march of Islamic militants across countries and continents. The Islamic State shows no sign of collapsing despite occasional setbacks in recent months, e.g., the loss of Falluja city and wresting of Manbij town by the Syria Democratic Forces dominated by Kurdish soldiers in the second week of August, 2016. ISIS has organized a fairly functional regime in the areas it controls by ruthlessly suppressing any potential opposition. By dint of hard work it has cobbled together a huge army of combat-ready warriors willing to die for establishing the supremacy of Islam worldwide. The current trends have the potential of consolidating the Islamic State as an independent Islamic country, altogether different from the universal concept of a nation State. The defeat of Islamic State can be ensured only by putting thousands of boots on the ground in West Asia and Africa. But that is an option which no nation is prepared to exercise. In any case, the truth about the need for massive boots on the ground has come to be accepted by almost all strategists.

Flashpoint India

Throughout history, jihad, or Islam's holy war against kaffirs, has been the battle cry of Muslim militant groups worldwide. The ISIS is no different. It has the same ideology and has adopted the same goals. It has built a State comprising vast territories and has a religion, too, which is euphemistically called the Religion of Peace. For Indians, the ongoing jihad whether waged by Pakistan, or the Indian Mujahideen, or for that matter by the Islamic State, is not something new. It is the same jihad which had ravaged and savaged Hindu civilization for nearly one thousand years. From the eighth century onwards, the storm-troopers of Islam had mercilessly slaughtered lakhs of innocents, plundered and destroyed thousands of temples, pillaged hundreds of cities and carried thousands, nay lakhs, of enslaved men and women across the Hindu Kush for sale in the slave markets of Ghazni, Kabul and Baghdad. Their sole objective was to destroy the Hindu civilization, root and branch.

Unfortunately we Indians (read somnolent Hindus) have battalions of secular chatterati wanting us to forget the one thousand year-long narrative of persecution and plunder by invaders and predators. They continue to churn deceptive stories like, 'Aman Ki Asha' and the Mughal-imposed culture called 'Ganga-Jamuni Tehzeeb' to dupe and befool the gullible Indian masses. Perhaps in the hearts of the sham-secular Indians, has been nurtured, wittingly or unwittingly, a death-wish. It is time that they realize that once the ISIS comes to India, all non-Muslims are likely to face the same old savagery, pock-marked by beheadings, forced conversions and violation of women, against which our forebears had fought. All jihadi groups like ISIS, Al Qaeda, Lashkar-e-Tayebba, Indian Mujahideen, SIMI, etc., have one common objective. Their goal is to overrun India and then defeat and destroy all non-Muslim nations. In the circumstances, at a suitable juncture, India may have to join France, Russia and other western powers in their war against the Islamic State and global jihadi terrorism. Concentrating on self-defense is not the best way to live in peace – unless we opt for the peace of the graveyard! A country of the size of India must have the daring to attack the enemy in its lair. As the largest democracy in the world it is also India's duty and responsibility to save humanity from the savagery of barbarians.

Even if Al-Baghdadi is killed, the global war of Islam against kaffirs of the world will continue. His place will be taken over by some other fiery campaigner of jihad who could be more ruthless. The Islamic street has a surfeit of killer bad boys. The ongoing global war could last for many more decades, even for the next twenty five or fifty years. That is a daunting prospect for all non-Muslim nations. The proof of pudding is in the eating thereof. Despite the killing of

Osama bin Laden by America's Navy Seals in May, 2011, global jihad has continued uninterrupted. That gives a clue to the shape of things to come in future.

Challenges For The Security Forces

The following important aspects of India's security preparedness ought to be thoroughly analyzed and debated by eminent security experts and intelligence agencies. Thereafter, a multi-pronged strategy should be evolved to defeat the threat posed by the Islamic State.

First and foremost, Central and the State governments must undertake a data-based appreciation of the threat posed by ISIS, Lashkar and allied groups, duly aided by Pakistan, including the multiple spy nests embedded in India. An evaluation should be made of the threats likely to emanate from our immediate neighborhood as well as West Asia. The action plan should take into account the possibility of sudden eruption of jihadi attacks simultaneously in many sensitive locations in various States.

The training of all para-military forces and police of various States should be revamped and massively upgraded with greater emphasis on incorporating exceptionally higher standards of physical fitness and combat efficiency. It's time to out match and beat the standards prescribed for ISIS foot soldiers in their online book, *The Black Flags from Islamic State.*

A critical review and upgradation of the regimen of training being imparted to the police forces of States as well as para-military forces, is absolutely essential. Among other things, tactical training should include the capacity to face the savagery and brutality being used by the ISIS, Al-Qaeda, Lashkar-e-Tayyeba, Indian Mujahideen, et al.

To defeat Abu Bakr Naji's vile strategy of creating pockets of 'vexation and exhaustion', all 'no-go' areas in every State and major city should be identified and listed district-wise and city-wise. A bold effort should be made to effectively prevent the creation of more such pockets. Strong steps should be taken to enforce strict police patrolling across all 'no-go' zones.

There is a special emphasis in Naji's war manual, *Management of Savagery*, on staging 'spectacular' attacks to demoralize the kaffirs. It is therefore essential to evolve a proper system of anticipating and defeating all such plans and manouvres. For foiling any attempted 'spectacular attacks' all State police forces should prepare and keep handy district-wise lists of important installations, religious institutions, sensitive towns and locations which could be targeted.

Short term as well long term Action Plans should be drawn up to counter the long term Islamic campaigns targeting India. In doing so tactical advice and technological help must be sought from the government of Israel which has a long and successful record of fighting Islamic militancy on more than one front.

A comprehensive evaluation of the manpower available with the State police forces and central para-military forces should be undertaken for winning the future war against multiple groups of Islamic militants. There is an urgent need for increasing the strength of security personnel and armed forces.

Time has come to review and upgrade the architecture of intelligence collection. A system of indepth 'threat analysis' by the Intelligence Bureau, the Research & Analysis Wing, all para-military forces and the intelligence wings of State police forces needs to be evolved. There is an urgent need for enforcing a system of post-operational debriefing of arrested jihadis and their accomplices and circulation of the information elicited thereby.

It is imperative to introduce a system of monitoring day-to-day postings on jihadi websites. This important task has to be performed by the intelligence agencies as well as the State Police forces. Wherever necessary, all provocative posts on Internet may be neutralized. Equally important, is the need to put in place a system of effective scrutiny of the departure and arrival by air or train of all persons having suspicious antecedents.

And if the frequent pronouncements by the likes of Baghdadi and the notorious Pak-based jihadis like Hafiz Saeed are to be believed, India will continue to be attacked again and again. The ongoing jihad to subjugate India will continue for decades, unless crushed with an iron hand. Labels of different Islamic groups are irrelevant. The Islamic State belongs to the same genre to which the Lashkar-e-Tayeba, Jaish-e-Mohammed, Indian Mujahideen, SIMI, Qaedat-al Qaeda and other anti-Indian outfits like the United Jihad Council and Jamaat-ul Mujahideen Bangladesh belong. It is a far more dangerous enemy and represents a daunting challenge to the Indian nation.

The repetitive threats issued by the Islamic State to attack India should not be considered as empty boasts. The danger is real and imminent. The Indian strategists must make earnest preparations to counter it. There is an urgent need for strategic deliberations on the subject and upgradation of our security architecture. But far more important is the need for enhancing manifold the physical stamina and combat efficiency of our security forces so that they can defeat the dangerous force multiplier of savagery.

EPILOGUE

The emergence of Islamic State has dramatically changed the geostrategic profile of the Middle East. It has successfully pockmarked the European continent and parts of Africa. The USA, a global super power, and its allies have failed to curb the fast-paced march of ISIS to distant lands and greener pastures. The warriors of ISIS are now embedded in more than dozens of countries. They are busy spewing violence across the globe through Military Affiliates called Wilayats.

Recently the Islamic State has suffered some setbacks including the loss of the strategic city of Falluja in Iraq and of Libya's coastal town of Sirte. But its sphere of influence across the globe has not diminished. A new classified document being studied by the White House contains a *'Heat Map'* which shows a stunning three-fold increase in the number of places around the world where ISIS is firmly established.[1] The document indicates that in 2014 when America launched its campaign against the Islamic State there were only seven nations in which the ISIS was operating. By July, 2015, however, the number increased to 13 countries. The latest data confirms that ISIS is now fully operational in 18 countries.

The document further highlights a new category described as "aspirational branches" of ISIS which lists countries where the jihadi group has struck roots. The six "aspirational" countries are Egypt, Mali, Bangladesh, Indonesia and the Philippines where terror attacks have been successfully carried out. These are aspirational regions where ISIS is trying to step up its violent activities, in the near future.

ISIS May Hit US Airbases in Mideast

According to an Israeli cyber intelligence group, ISIS has issued a specific call to its activists to target the air bases used by the USA in Kuwait, Bahrain and Saudi Arabia.[2] The Israeli company which is run by former intelligence officers of Israeli Defence Force (IDF) claimed to have gathered the important information by hacking the jihadi outfit's *Telegram* group on the dark web. The said *Telegramgroup* disseminates plans for terrorist attacks among 500 leading actvists of Islamic State.

Recently William McCants, Senior Fellow, Foreign Policy Center for Middle East, warned against celebrating the setbacks to ISIS.[3] He argues that there is an impression in the strategic community that the Islamic State's legitimacy would be damaged if it lost its government, implying loss of territory. It is felt that a state without a state would become a laughing stock. But that may not happen soon. If the Islamic group's previous incarnations are any indication, the laughter might come only after a generation. That means the battle against the holy warriors could last 25 long years. He recalls that the Islamic State had suffered ridicule for its out sized ambitions earlier also. When Al-Qaida in Iraq was dissolved in 2006 and establishment of Islamic State of Iraq was announced, many had scoffed. It was pointed out how could a rebel group that controlled a small territory claim that it was an actual state? The Islamic State's rejoinder was that it was a state because it was trying to behave like a state by promising to endure against all odds. Ultimately the previous incarnation of Islamic State did manage to emerge as an independent entity.

Endnotes

Introduction

1. Gopal Das Khosla, Stern Reckoning, *The Partition Omnibus, Oxford University Press,* Appendix I, p. 303, New Delhi, 2002.

Chapter 1

1. Yasmin Al-Khatib, *MEMRI Special Dispatch No. 6144,* August 28, 2015.
2. Ibid.
3. Egyptian TV Host Ibrahim Issa: Nobody Dares to Admit that ISIS Crimes are Based on Islamic Sources, *Middle East Media Research Institute,* February 3, 2015.
4. Ibid.
5. Abu Bakr Naji, *Management of Savagery* (translated into English by William Mc Cants) p. 11.
6. Ibid.
7. Samuel Oakford, 'Number of Foreign Fighters Who Travelled to Syria and Iraq Doubled Since Last Year', *Soufan Group,* December 9, 2015.
8. Katie Zavadski, 'ISIS now has a network of Military Affiliates in 11 countries around the world', *Daily Intelligencer,* November 23, 2014.
9. Tamer El-Ghobashy and Hassan Morajea, 'Islamic State Tightens Grip on Libyan Stronghold of Sirte', *The Wall Street Journal,* November 29, 2016.
10. *Agence France Presse,* ISIS gaining ground in Afghanistan: UN, *the Daily Star,* Lebanon, Sept. 6, 2015.

11. Louella Mae Eleftheriou Smith, *Global Terrorism Index*, 'Over 42 militant groups have pledged allegiance to ISIS', *Times of India World Website*, December 10, 2015 (*timesofindia.indiatimes.com/world/middle- east/Global Terrorism-Index-The-map-that shows-where-42 different- militant-groups-have pledged-support*).

12. Cristina Silva, 'ISIS Expanding in African Nations after Jahba East Africa Pledges Allegiance to Islamic State Leader Abu Bakr Al-Baghdadi', *International Business Times*, April 8, 2016.

13. Stuart Ramsay, Chief Correspondent, SKY News, 'IS Registration Forms identify 22,000 jihadis', *pamelageller.com /2016/03/isis-registration-forms-identify-22000-jihadis.html*, and *mail online website*, August 19, 2016.

14. Ibid.

15. Samuel Oakford, 'Number of Foreign Fighters Who Travelled to Syria and Iraq Doubled Since Last Year', *Soufan Group*, December 9, 2015.

16. Dr. B.R. Ambedkar, *Pakistan or Partition of India*, p. 39.

17. Islamic State's regional strategy, *European Council of Foreign Affairs,www.ecfr.eu/article/community_the_islamic_states_strategy*.

18. News item 'At $2.4 bn ISIS is still richest group', *Times of India*, New Delhi, June 3, 2016, p.24.

19. Shiv Malik, 'ISIS Papers: Leaked documents show how ISIS is building its state', *The Guardian*, London, 7 December, 2015.

20. Source: *The Jerusalem Times*, August 30, 2015.

21. Will Stewart and Simon Tomlinson, 'Putin signs decree drafting conscripts into the Russian military', *Mail Online*, October 2, 2015.

22. Shereena Qazi, ISIL hits Afghan airwaves to drum up support, Aljazeera.com

23. Edwin Mora, 'Voice of Caliphate', Islamic State in Afghanistan Launches Radio Station, *Breitbart News*, Washington, 19 December, 2015.

24. Michael S. Schimidt, 'USA steps up airstrikes against ISIS after it gains Territory in Afghanistan', *The New York Times*, March 16, 2016.

Chapter 2

1. The Crimes of Palmyra http//*www.nytimes.com/2015/08/26/opinion/the- crimes of palmyra.html.*

2. Ibid.

3. Donatella Rovera, *www.amnesty.org/Iraq.*

4. Richard Spencer, Middle East Editor, Islamic State Jihadist executes own mother in public. *The Telegraph*, London, January 8, 2016.

5. ISIS executes 2 doctors in Central Mosul, *Iraqi News*, www.iraqinews.com

6. Alain Jocard, AFP, www.dailymail.co./uk/I-want-blue-eyed-yazidi-teen-describes-is-scare-m, September 2, 2015.

7. Christine Williams, *Fox News*, June 7, 2016.

8. The Clarion Project, a news item - ISIS Massacres Nuns in Yemen, March 20, 2016, *www.clarionproject.org*

9. Ibid.

10. Phillip Sherwell, Islamic State jihadis threaten to behead western hostages, *Telegraph*, April 24, 2016.

11. Ibid.

Chapter 3

1. *Breitbart News Network,* Jerusalem, 'Top Jihadist Claims Islamic State has agents working in western airports', March 25, 2016.

2. Ibid.

3. Ibid.

4. Gopal Das Khosla, *Stern Reckoning, The Partition Omnibus,* published by Oxford University Press, p. 49.
5. Rowan Scarborough, *The Washington Times,* July 13, 2016.

Chapter 4

1. G. Parthasarthy, Pakistani Army, Loot at Sight, *The Pioneer,* New Delhi, August 14, 2003.
2. Pramod Kumar Singh – Pak nurses three, not one designs on India, *The Pioneer,* New Delhi, August 28, 2003.
3. Sara A. Carter, Islamic State recruitment document seeks to provoke 'End of world', American Media Institute, July 28, 2015.
4. Carol Anne Grayson, 'Islamic State: Plan to develop Wilayat Hind (Province of India)', Radical Sister Blog, January 16, 2016.
5. Ibid.
6. Saroj Kumar Rath, 'India's terror threat growing: Al-Qaeda chief Ayaman al Zawahari appointed head of a new outfit to attack India', Yale Global online, 20 November, 2014.
7. Ibid.
8. Ibid.
9. Sumit Kumar Singh, 'Delhi Cops Bust ISIS Terror Recruitment Racket', *the New Indian Express,* New Delhi, January 16, 2016.
10. Source: News item 'Court sends 12 terror suspects to NIA custody till February 5', The *Tribune,* New Delhi, PTI, January 25, 201
11. Brigadier S.K. Malik, *the Quranic Concept of War,* pp. 59-60.
12. Ibid.
13. Samuel Oakford, 'Number of Foreign Fighters who Travelled to Syria and Iraq Doubled since Last Year', soufangroup.com.
14. Tom Cheshire, Islamic State Files: 'Goldmine of Information' *Sky News,* March 10, 2016
15. Ibid.

Chapter 5

1. Taruni Kumar, Observer Research Foundation http://www.orfonline.org/cms/expot/orfonline/modules/isuebrief/a ttachments/ Issue Brief92_1433826472805/pdf/]
2. Ibid.
3. 'Marathi daily *Lokmat* attacked by Muslims for publishing a derogatory; illustration, *Agency*. *DNA web desk*, Monday 30 November, 2015.
4. M.L. Kak, 'Where is the Thaw', *The Tribune*, Chandigarh, February 9, 2002.
5. Ibid.
6. Sagnik Chowdhury, Oct. 18, 2015, 'Named by 'IS recruiter Afshan Jabeen, nine under scanner', *indianexpress.com/article/ india-news- india]*
7. Thamizhchelvan, 'Tamil Nadu in the grip of Jihad'. Vijayavaani.com, 28 April, 2016.
8. NDT Bureau, 'ISIS and LeT Join Hands' *New Delhi Times,* 3-9 August, 2015, p. 3.
9. Ibid.
10. Smriti Singh, 'Bhatkal wanted to carry out fedayeen attacks on train with foreign passengers in 2011, *Economic Times,* New Delhi, March 2, 2013.

Chapter 6

1. Animesh Roul, Ansar-ut-Tawhid and the Transnational Threat to India, The *Jamestown Terrorism Monitor*, 13th June, 2014.
2. Ryan Mauro, Exclusive: Terror Org. Harbored by Pakistani Govt. Now Backs ISIS, *The Clarion Project*, December 29, 2014.
3. Tufail Ahmed, 'The threat of Islamic Radicalization in India', indiafacts.org, March 30, 2015.
4 . Ibid.
5. Ibid.

6. Speech by Marine Le Pen to the EU Parliament on Islamic terrorism, *Bare Naked Islam*.

7. Sierra Rayne's Blog, 'Pew Poll, Between 63 million and 287 million ISIS supporters in just 11 countries', American Thinker, November 18, 2015.

8. Ibid.

9. Hana Levi Julian, 'Phone Transcripts Evoke Horror of Mumbai Attacks', Artuz Sheva, israelnationalnews.com.

10. Santosh Mishra, 'New Horror: Terrorists humiliated guests before killing them', *All Mirrors,* Mumbai, December 25, 2008.

Chapter 7

1. S. Hussain Zaidi, 'The 100 hours Op to catch 12 Maldivians Leaving to Join ISIS', *Mumbai Mirror*, April 22, 2016.

2. Source: *Black Flags from the Islamic State, How al-Qaidah became the IslamicState,* www.investigativeproject.org/documents/misc/864.pdf].

3. Ambika.Pandit@timesgroup.com, *Sunday Times*, New Delhi, 22nd May 2016, pp. 1 and 4].

4. Ritesh K. Srivastava, *Zee Media Bureau*, August 8, 2016.

Chapter 8

1. Wikipedia, the free international encyclopedia.

2. Ibid.

3. Tony Blair, www.tonyblairoffice.org/...../why the-middle-east-matters-Keynote speech.

4. Ibid.

5. Ibid.

Epilogue

1. William Arkin, Robert Windrem and Cynthia Mcfadden, NBC News, August 3, 2016.

2. By Times of Israel staff, www.timesofisrael.com/israel-company-claims-hack-on-is-chat-group-with-list-of-future-targets, August 3, 2016].

3. William McCants, *Senior Fellow, Foreign Policy Center for Middle East*, Brookings Institution, 'Don't celebrate ISIS setbacks too soon', August 9, 2016.

Index

APPENDIX

Global Affiliates of Islamic State

The following 63 Islamic groups have pledged allegiance and support to Islamic State :

1. Ansar al-Tawhid in India [Pledged Allegiance in October, 2014],
2. Wilayat Khorasan – created to target India and Pakistan [Allegiance: August, 2015].
3. Wilayat Hind – created to target India [Allegiance: September, 2015].
4. Al-Hind Brigade of Maldives – created to target India [Allegiance: April, 2016].
5. Abu Sayyaf Group of Philippines [Allegiance: July, 2014].
6. Ansar al-Khilafah of Philippines [Allegiance: August, 2014].
7. Al-Huda Battalion in Maghreb of Islam (Algeria) [Allegiance: June, 2014].
8. Ansar Al-Sharia Libya & Tunisia [Allegiance: August, 2014].
9. Al-I'tisam of Koran and Sunnah of Sudan [Allegiance: August, 2014].
10. Bangsamoro Islamic Freedom Fighters of Phillippines [Allegiance: August, 2014].
11. Bangsmoro Justice Movement of Phillippines [Allegiance: September, 2014].
12. Jemaah Islamiyah (Philippines) [Allegiance: April, 2015].
13. The Soldiers of the Caliphate in Algeria [Allegiance: September, 2014].
14. Al-Ghurabaa (Algeria) [Allegiance: July, 2015].

15. Djamaat Houmat ad-Da'wa as-Salafiya (DHDS) of Algeria [Allegiance: Sept., 2015].
16. Al-Ansar Battalion (Algeria) [Allegiance: September, 2014].
17. Jundullah (Pakistan) [Allegiance: November, 2014].
18. Islamic Movement of Uzbekistan (IMU) (Pakistan/Uzbekistan) [Allegiance: September, 2014].
19. Leaders of Mujahids in Khorasan (ten former TTP commanders) – Pakistan [Allegiance: January, 2015].
20. Jaish al-Sahabah in the Levant [Allegiance : July, 2014].
21. Islamic Youth Shura Council (Libya) [Allegiance: June, 2014].
22. Martyrs of al-Yarmouk Brigade (Syria) [Allegiance: December, 2014].
23. Katibat al-Imam Bukhari (Syria) [Allegiance: October, 2014].
24. Jund al-Khilafah in Egypt [Allegiance: September, 2014].
25. Liwa Ahrar al-Sunna in Baalbek (Lebanon) [Allegiance: July, 2014].
26. Islamic State Libya (Darnah) [Allegiance : November, 2014].
27. Lions of Libya [Allegiance: September, 2014].
28. Shura Council of Shabab al-Islam Darnah (Libya) [Allegiance: October, 2014].
29. Jemaah Anshorut Tauhid (JAT) (Indonesia) [Allegiance: June, 2014]
30. Mujahideen Indonesia Timor (MIT) (Indonesia) [Allegiance: July, 2014].
31. Ansar al-Khliafah of The Philippines [Allegiance: 2014].
32. Al-Qaeda in the Islamic Maghreb, Algeria and Mali [Allegiance: July, 2014].
33. Ansar Bayt al-Maqdis (now known as Wilayat Sinai of Islamic State) Gaza Strip [Allegiance: November, 2014].
34. Bangsamoro Islamic Freedom Fighters of The Philippines [Allegiance: August, 2014]

35. Boko Haram, Nigeria and Lake Chad Basin [Allegiance: March, 2015].

36. Caucasus Emirate (Wilayat Caucasus) [Allegiance: June, 2015].

37. Islamic Movement of Uzbekistan [Allegiance: September, 2014].

38. Hezb-e-Islami, Afghanistan Formed [Allegiance: July, 2015].

39. Islamic Youth Shura Council, Libya [Allegiance: October, 2014].

40. Jemaah Islamiyah, Malaysia, Thailand, Singapore, Brunei & Indonesia [Allegiance: August, 2014].

41. Jund al-Khilafah, Algeria and Egypt [Allegiance: September, 2014].

42. Katibat UqbahIbn Nafaa, Tunisia [Allegiance: September, 2014].

43. Mujahideen Shura Council in Environs of Jerusalem, Egypt and the Gaza [Allegiance: September, 2014].

44. Tehreek-e-Taliban Pakistan (former PakistaniTaliban) [Allegiance: October, 2014].

45. Tehreek-e-Khilafat, Pakistan [Allegiance: July, 2014].

46. Okba Ibn Nafaa Battalion [Tunisia] [Allegiance: Sept., 2014].

47. Jund al-Khilafah in Tunisia [Allegiance March, 2015].

48. Central Sector of Kabardino-Balakria of Caucasus Emirate, Russia [Allegiance April, 2015].

49. Mujahideen of Tunisia of Kairouan [Allegiance May, 2015].

50. Mujahideen of Yemen [Allegiance Nov., 2014].

51. Supporters of the Islamic State in Yemen [Allegiance : Sept., 2014].

52. Al-Tawheed Brigade in Khorasan (Afghanistan) [Alllegiance : Sept., 2014].

53. Heroes of Islam Brigade in Khorasan (Afghanistan) [Allegiance: Sept., 2014].

54. Supporters of Islamic State in the Land of Two Holy Mosques (Saudi Arabia) [Allegiance: October, 2014].

55. Ansar al-Islam (Iraq) [Allegiance: January, 2015].

56. Nokhcho Wilayat of the Caucasus Emirate (CE) (Russia) [Allegiance: June, 2015].

57. Al-Ansar Battalion (Algeria) [Allegiance: Sept., 2015].

58. Al-Shabaab Jubba Region Cell of Bashir Abu Numan (Somalia) [Allegiance: Dec., 2015].

59. Ansarullah Bangla of Bangladesh [Date of allegiance to ISIS not known].

60. Ansarullah Bahini of Bangladesh. [Date of announcing allegiance to ISIS not known].

61. Jamiat-ul-Salafi of Maldives [Date of swearing allegiance to ISIS not known].

62. Ansar-al-Khilafah Brazil created to target Brazil and Latin America [Allegiance : July, 2016].

63. Junod-al Khalifah-al Hind created to target India [Allegiance : March, 2016].

The above mentioned list of global Affiliates of the Islamic State has been compiled from a number of sources including articles, documents and the data posted on a number of websites on Internet. Some of these Affiliates are hyper-active, while others are dormant. A few Affiliates like Wilayat Hind, Al-Hind Brigade of Maldives and Jamiat-ul Salafi of Maldives are works in progress.

www.ingramcontent.com/pod-product-compliance
Lightning Source LLC
Chambersburg PA
CBHW052127270326
41930CB00012B/2789